Teacher Edition

Planning Guide

fusion [FYOO • zhuhn] a combination of two or more things that releases energy

HOUGHTON MIFFLIN HARCOURT

Front Cover: *stingray* ©Jeffrey L. Rotman/Corbis; *moth* ©Millard H. Sharp/Photo Researchers, Inc.; *astronaut* ©NASA; *thermometer* ©StockImages/Alamy; *robotic arm* ©Garry Gay/The Image Bank/Getty Images

Back Cover: *rowers* ©Stockbyte/Getty Images; *beaker* ©Gregor Schuster/Getty Images; *tree frog* ©DLILLC/Corbis; *Great Basin National Park* ©Frans Lanting/Corbis

Printed in the U.S.A.

ISBN 978-0-547-69694-2

6 7 8 9 10 0877 20 19 18 17 16 15 14 13

4500414032 CDEFG

Planning Guide Contents

Consulting Authors

Michael A. DiSpezio

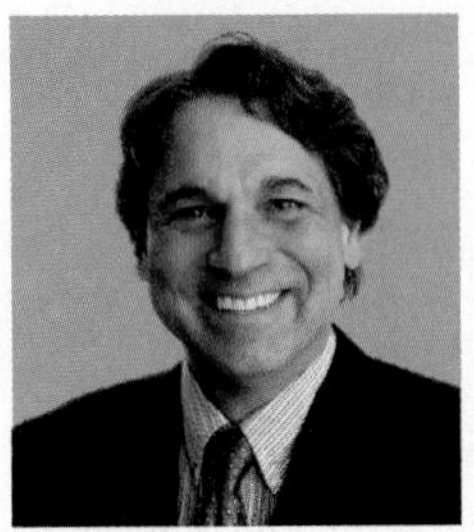

Global Educator
North Falmouth, Massachusetts

Michael DiSpezio is a renaissance educator who segued from the research laboratory of a Nobel Prize winner to the K–12 science classroom. He has authored or co-authored numerous textbooks and trade books. For nearly a decade he worked with the JASON Project, under the auspices of the National Geographic Society, where he designed curriculum, wrote lessons, and hosted dozens of studio and location broadcasts. Over the past two decades, DiSpezio has developed supplementary material for organizations and programs that include PBS Scientific American Frontiers, *Discover* Magazine, and the Discovery Channel. To all his projects, he brings his extensive background in science and his expertise in classroom teaching at the elementary, middle, and high school levels.

Marjorie Frank

Science Writer and Content-Area Reading Specialist
Brooklyn, New York

An educator and linguist by training, a writer and poet by nature, Marjorie Frank has authored and designed a generation of instructional materials in all subject areas, including past HMH Science programs. Her other credits include authoring science issues of an award-winning children's magazine; writing game-based digital assessments in math, reading, and language arts; and serving as instructional designer and co-author of pioneering school-to-work software for a nonprofit organization dedicated to improving reading and math skills for middle and high school learners. In addition, she has served on the adjunct faculty of Hunter, Manhattan, and Brooklyn Colleges, teaching courses in science methods, literacy, and writing.

Michael R. Heithaus

Director, School of Environment and Society
Associate Professor, Department of Biological Sciences
Florida International University
North Miami, Florida

Mike Heithaus joined the Florida International University Biology Department in 2003, has served as Director of the Marine Sciences Program, and is now Director of the School of Environment and Society, which brings together the natural and social sciences and humanities to develop solutions to today's environmental challenges. His research efforts include the Shark Bay Ecosystem Project in Western Australia. He also served as a Research Fellow with National Geographic, using remote imaging in his research and hosting a *Crittercam* television series on the National Geographic Channel. His current research centers on predator-prey interactions among vertebrates.

Donna M. Ogle

Professor of Reading and Language
National-Louis University
Chicago, Illinois

Creator of the well-known KWL strategy, Donna Ogle has directed many staff development projects translating theory and research into school practice in schools throughout the United States. She is a past president of the International Reading Association and has served as a consultant on literacy projects worldwide. Her extensive international experience includes coordinating the Reading and Writing for Critical Thinking Project in Eastern Europe and speaking and consulting on projects in several Latin American countries and in Asia. Her books include *Reading Comprehension: Strategies for Independent Learners; All Children Read;* and *Literacy for a Democratic Society.*

Program Advisors

Paul D. Asimow
Professor of Geology and Geochemistry
California Institute of Technology
Pasadena, California

Bobby Jeanpierre
Associate Professor of Science Education
University of Central Florida
Orlando, Florida

Gerald H. Krockover
Professor of Earth and Atmospheric Science Education
Purdue University
West Lafayette, Indiana

Rose Pringle
Associate Professor
School of Teaching and Learning
College of Education
University of Florida
Gainesville, Florida

Carolyn Staudt
Curriculum Designer for Technology
KidSolve, Inc./The Concord Consortium
Concord, Massachusetts

Larry Stookey
Science Department
Antigo High School
Antigo, Wisconsin

Carol J. Valenta
Associate Director of the Museum and Senior Vice President
Saint Louis Science Center
St. Louis, Missouri

Barry A. Van Deman
President and CEO
Museum of Life and Science
Durham, North Carolina

Classroom Reviewers

Surbhi Madia Barber
Cottage Grove Elementary
Cottage Grove, Wisconsin

Michael J. Bodek
Green Ridge Elementary
Mechanicsburg, Pennsylvania

Abby Cunningham
Anderson Island Elementary
Anderson Island, Washington

Mark T. Esch
Cottage Grove Elementary
Cottage Grove, Wisconsin

Tina M. Gilbert
Cottage Grove Elementary
Cottage Grove, Wisconsin

Timothy J. Gollup
Cottage Grove Elementary
Cottage Grove, Wisconsin

A J Hepworth
Mineola Middle School
Mineola, New York

Wendy Hughes
Cottage Grove Elementary
Cottage Grove, Wisconsin

Nan Kaufman
Livonia Public Schools
Livonia, Michigan

Diane S. Kohl
M.J. Gegan Elementary School
Menasha, Wisconsin

Joseph C. Kubasta
Rockwood Valley MS
Wildwood, Missouri

Dustin C. LeBlanc
Sporting Hill Elementary
Mechanicsburg, Pennsylvania

Susanne Moar
Rockwood School District
Science Department
Eureka, Missouri

Pamela Pauling
Wheatland Elementary
Andover, Kansas

Allen G. Rauch
Associate Professor of Science Education
Molloy College
Rockville Centre, New York

Tim Rupp
Gordon Elementary
Marshall, Michigan

Michelle A. Salgado
National Board Certified Teacher
Chloe Clark Elementary
DuPont, Washington

Brent Schacht
Cottage Grove Elementary
Cottage Grove, Wisconsin

Power up with SCIENCE FUSION

Print

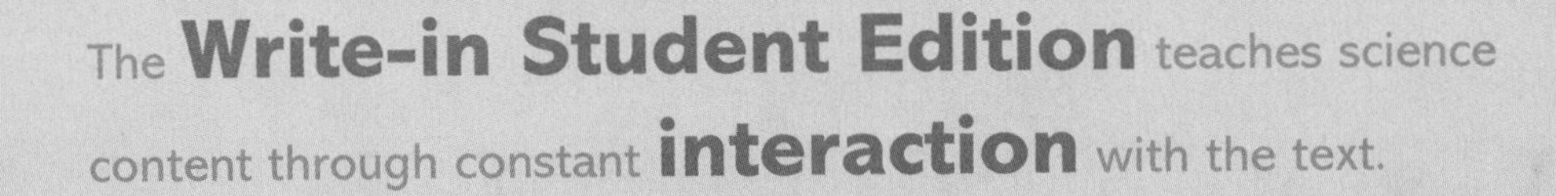

The **Write-in Student Edition** teaches science content through constant **interaction** with the text.

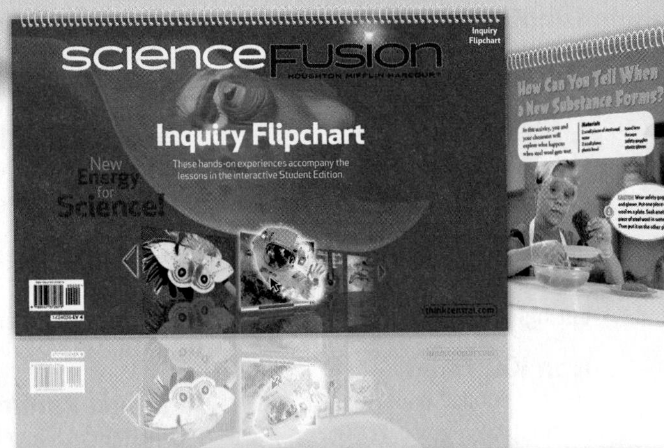

Labs and Activities

Digital

The parallel **Digital Curriculum** provides **e-learning digital lessons and virtual labs** for every print lesson of the program.

Energize your students through a multi-modal blend of Print, Inquiry, and Digital experiences.

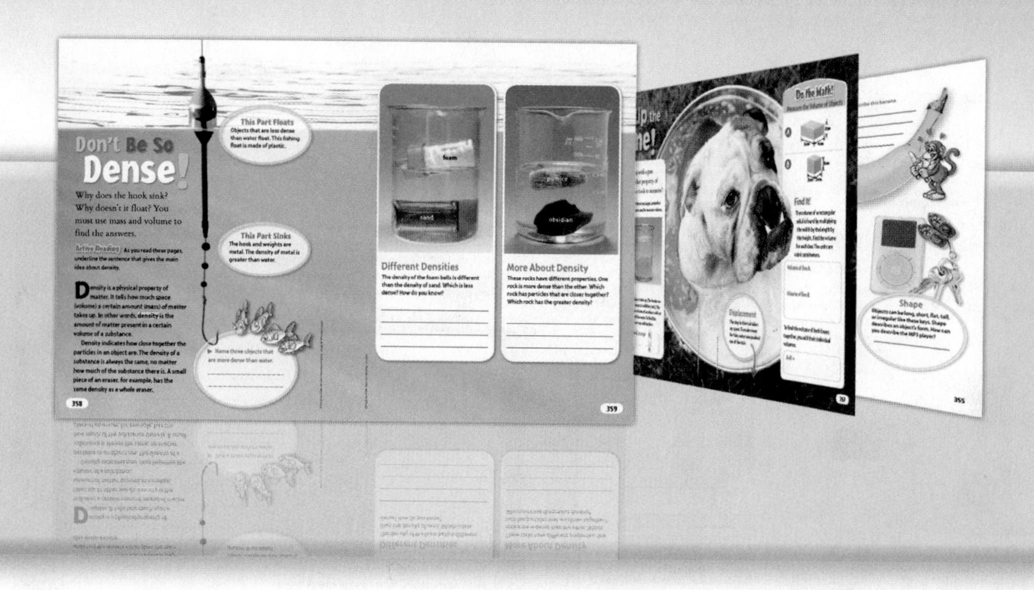

The **Inquiry Flipchart** and **Virtual Labs** provide meaningful and exciting hands-on experiences.

Assessment

Formative Assessment

Student Edition
- Sum It Up!
- Brain Check

Summative Assessment

Student Edition
- Unit Review

Assessment Guide
- Lesson Quizzes
- Unit Test

Performance Assessment

SHORT OPTION: Teacher Edition

LONG OPTION: Assessment Guide

RTI Response to Intervention

RTI Strategies

Online Assessment

Test-taking and automatic scoring

Banks of items from which to build tests

Print

The **Write-in Student Edition** teaches science content through constant **interaction** with the text.

Write-in Student Edition

The *ScienceFusion* write-in student edition promotes a student-centered approach for

- learning science concepts and vocabulary
- building inquiry, STEM, and 21st Century skills
- incorporating math and writing in each science lesson

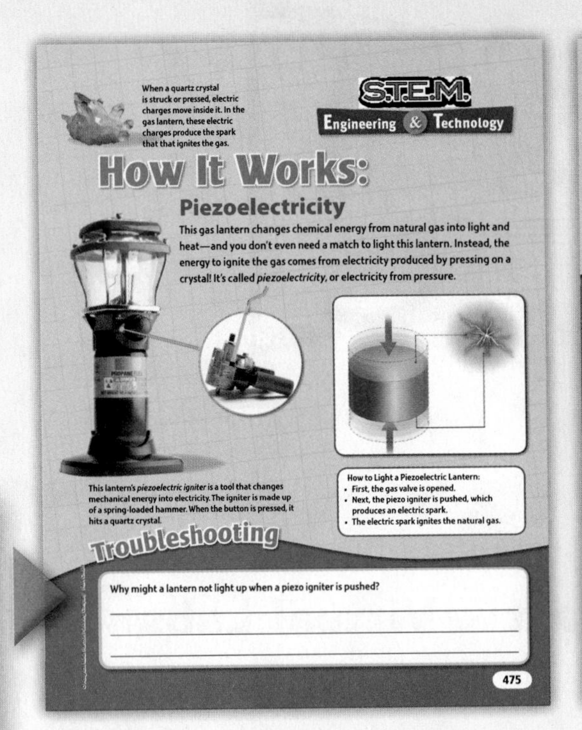

When a quartz crystal is struck or pressed, electric charges move inside it. In the gas lantern, these electric charges produce the spark that that ignites the gas.

S.T.E.M. Engineering & Technology

How It Works: Piezoelectricity

This gas lantern changes chemical energy from natural gas into light and heat—and you don't even need a match to light this lantern. Instead, the energy to ignite the gas comes from electricity produced by pressing on a crystal! It's called *piezoelectricity*, or electricity from pressure.

This lantern's *piezoelectric igniter* is a tool that changes mechanical energy into electricity. The igniter is made up of a spring-loaded hammer. When the button is pressed, it hits a quartz crystal.

How to Light a Piezoelectric Lantern:
- First, the gas valve is opened.
- Next, the piezo igniter is pushed, which produces an electric spark.
- The electric spark ignites the natural gas.

Troubleshooting

Why might a lantern not light up when a piezo igniter is pushed?

475

S.T.E.M. continued

Solar cells *transform*, or change, solar energy into electricity. This electricity is transformed again as heat or light in a home.

Show How It Works

The gas lantern shows some ways energy changes take place. Mechanical energy changed into electrical energy, which ignited the natural gas. Chemical energy stored in the gas changed into heat and light. Identify different types of energy and their sources in your classroom or home. In the space below, draw and describe how energy from one of these sources is transformed.

Suppose that popcorn kernels are being cooked over a campfire. Describe the types of energy being used and how these types of energy change.

Build On It!

Rise to the engineering design challenge—complete **Solar Water Heater** on the Inquiry Flipchart.

476

S.T.E.M. Engineering & Technology

ScienceFusion features a STEM unit that focuses on

- engineering and technology
- learning science concepts and vocabulary
- building inquiry, STEM, and 21st Century skills

Big Ideas & Essential Questions

Each unit is designed to focus on a Big Idea and supporting Essential Questions.

Graphic Organizers

As they read, students summarize and organize their science ideas in charts, tables, diagrams, and other graphic organizers.

Active Reading

Annotation prompts and questions throughout the text teach students how to analyze and interact with content.

Do the Math!

Students practice and apply math skills as they are doing science.

Interactive Glossary

Students deepen their understanding of vocabulary by adding their own notes and context to glossary definitions.

ScienceFusion's multimodal approach connects a hands-on experience to the STEM lesson in the student edition.

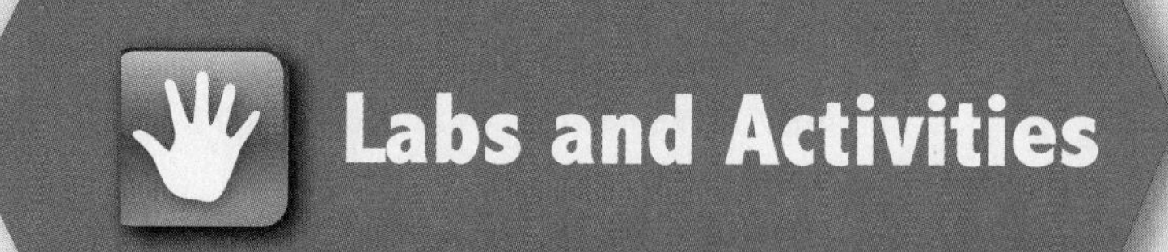

The **Inquiry Flipchart** and **Virtual Labs** provide meaningful and exciting hands-on experiences.

360° of Inquiry

Labs and Activities

Inquiry Flipcharts

The inquiry flipcharts deliver three levels—directed, guided, and independent—of hands-on inquiry for every lesson. The laminated, 11 x 17 flipcharts, also available digitally, can be placed on a table for centers or small group areas so students can work as lab partners or in collaborative groups.

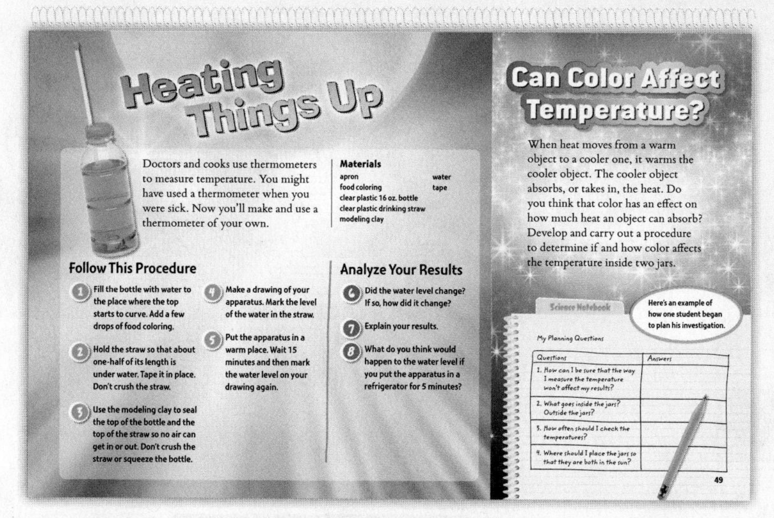

Heating Things Up

Doctors and cooks use thermometers to measure temperature. You might have used a thermometer when you were sick. Now you'll make and use a thermometer of your own.

Materials
apron, food coloring, clear plastic 16 oz. bottle, clear plastic drinking straw, modeling clay, water, tape

Follow This Procedure

1. Fill the bottle with water to the place where the top starts to curve. Add a few drops of food coloring.
2. Hold the straw so that about one-half of its length is under water. Tape it in place. Don't crush the straw.
3. Use the modeling clay to seal the top of the bottle and the top of the straw so no air can get in or out. Don't crush the straw or squeeze the bottle.
4. Make a drawing of your apparatus. Mark the level of the water in the straw.
5. Put the apparatus in a warm place. Wait 15 minutes and then mark the water level on your drawing again.

Analyze Your Results

6. Did the water level change? If so, how did it change?
7. Explain your results.
8. What do you think would happen to the water level if you put the apparatus in a refrigerator for 5 minutes?

Can Color Affect Temperature?

When heat moves from a warm object to a cooler one, it warms the cooler object. The cooler object absorbs, or takes in, the heat. Do you think that color has an effect on how much heat an object can absorb? Develop and carry out a procedure to determine if and how color affects the temperature inside two jars.

Science Notebook

Here's an example of how one student began to plan his investigation.

My Planning Questions

Questions	Answers
1. How can I be sure that the way I measure the temperature won't affect my results?	
2. What goes inside the jars? Outside the jars?	
3. How often should I check the temperature?	
4. Where should I place the jars so that they are both in the sun?	

49

Directed or Independent Inquiry

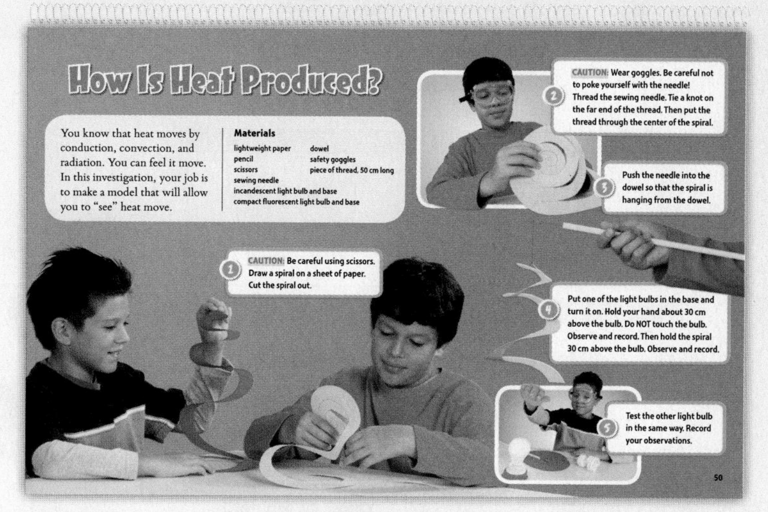

How Is Heat Produced?

You know that heat moves by conduction, convection, and radiation. You can feel it move. In this investigation, your job is to make a model that will allow you to "see" heat move.

Materials
lightweight paper, pencil, scissors, sewing needle, incandescent light bulb and base, compact fluorescent light bulb and base, dowel, safety goggles, piece of thread, 50 cm long

1. CAUTION: Be careful using scissors. Draw a spiral on a sheet of paper. Cut the spiral out.
2. CAUTION: Wear goggles. Be careful not to poke yourself with the needle! Thread the sewing needle. Tie a knot on the far end of the thread. Then put the thread through the center of the spiral.
3. Push the needle into the dowel so that the spiral is hanging from the dowel.
4. Put one of the light bulbs in the base and turn it on. Hold your hand about 30 cm above the bulb. Do NOT touch the bulb. Observe and record. Then hold the spiral 30 cm above the bulb. Observe and record.
5. Test the other light bulb in the same way. Record your observations.

50

Guided Inquiry

Inquiry Lesson and Virtual Lab

Each inquiry lesson in the student edition has a corresponding virtual lab to provide a multimodal approach for learning science concepts and skills.

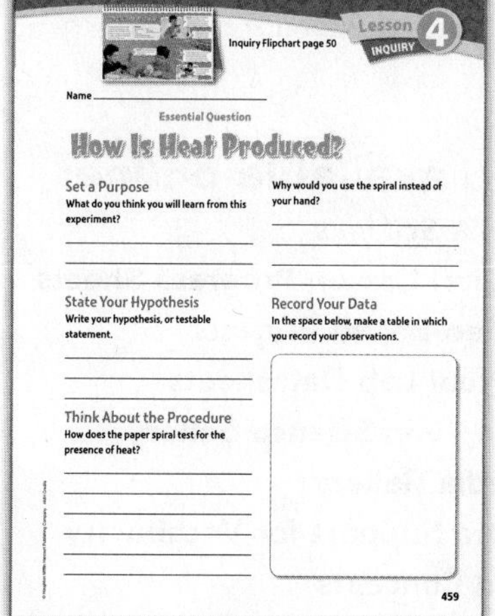

Inquiry Flipchart page 50

Lesson 4 INQUIRY

Name

Essential Question

How Is Heat Produced?

Set a Purpose
What do you think you will learn from this experiment?

Why would you use the spiral instead of your hand?

State Your Hypothesis
Write your hypothesis, or testable statement.

Record Your Data
In the space below, make a table in which you record your observations.

Think About the Procedure
How does the paper spiral test for the presence of heat?

459

Draw Conclusions
Was your hypothesis supported? Why or why not?

What conclusions can you draw about light sources and heat?

Analyze and Extend
1. What did you learn from this procedure about the difference between compact fluorescent bulbs and ordinary light bulbs?
2. Ordinary light bulbs use more electrical energy than compact fluorescent bulbs do. Why do you think this is so?
3. What other materials could you test in this way to see if they produce heat?
4. What other questions do you have about heat transfer?

460

Inquiry lesson

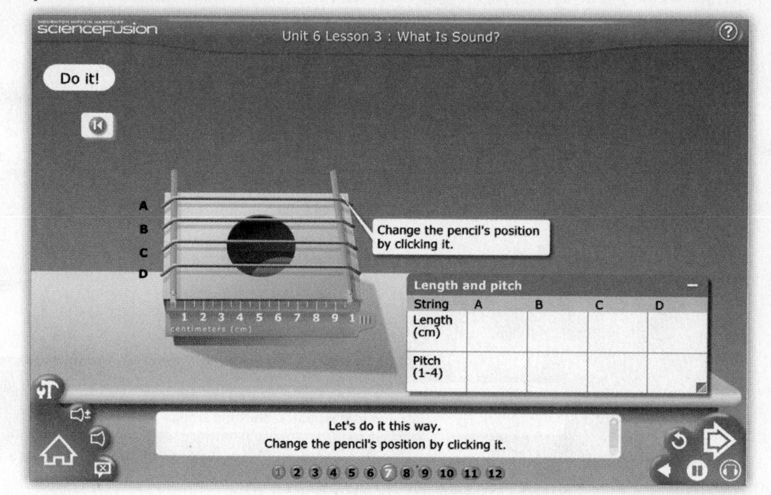

Virtual Lab

The parallel **Digital Curriculum** provides
e-learning digital lessons and virtual labs
for every print lesson of the program.

360° of Inquiry

Digital Lessons and Virtual Labs

An e-Learning environment of interactivity, videos, simulations, animations, and assessment designed for the way digital natives learn. An online Student Edition provides students anytime access to their student book.

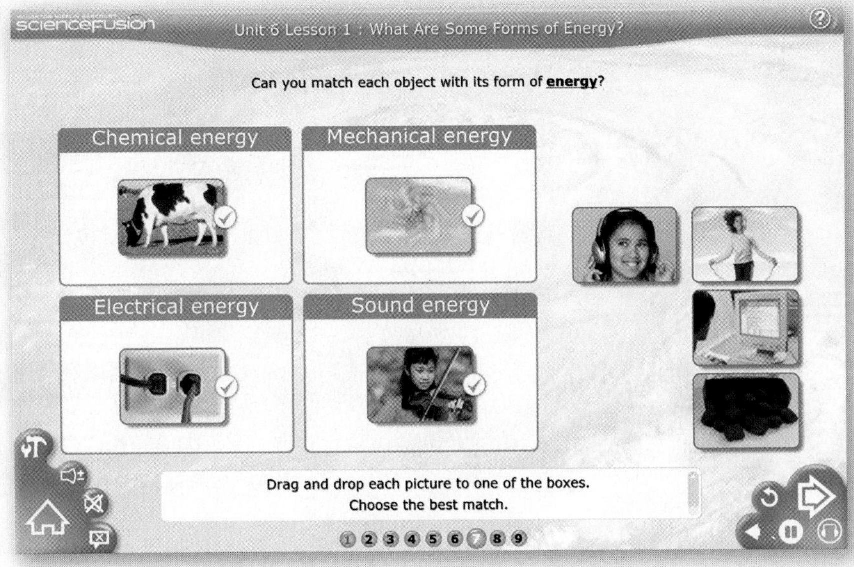

Digital Lessons

Online Student Edition

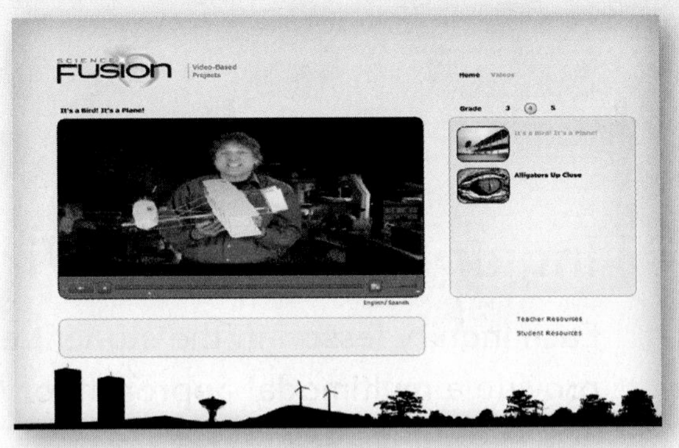

Video-Based Projects

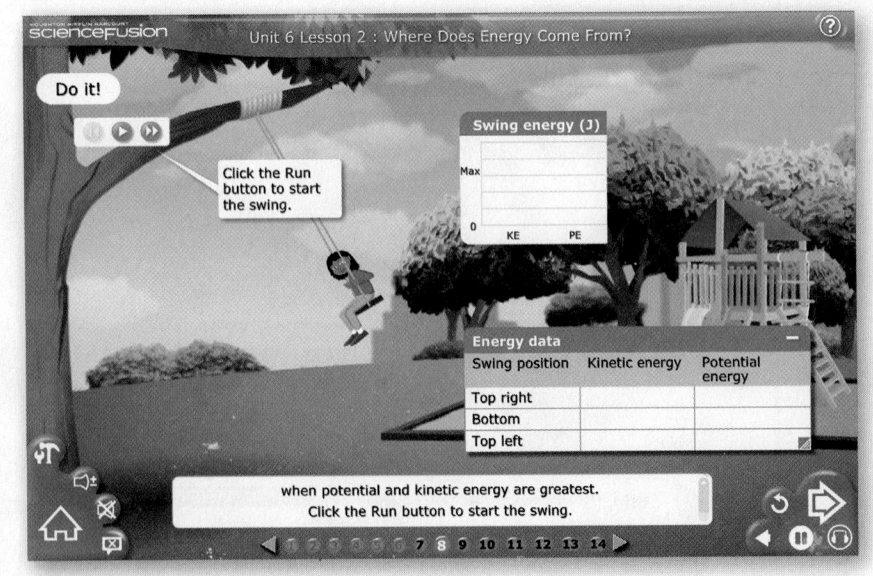

Virtual Labs

Also available online:

- NSTA *SciLinks*
- Digital Lesson Progress Sheets
- Video-Based Projects
- Virtual Lab Datasheets
- People in Science Gallery
- Media Gallery
- Extra Support for Vocabulary and Concepts
- Leveled Readers

All paths lead to a full suite of print and online **Assessment Options** right at your fingertips.

Classroom Management
Integrated Assessment Options

The *ScienceFusion* assessment options give you maximum flexibility in assessing what your students know and what they can do. Both the Print and Digital paths include formative and summative assessment. See the **Assessment Guide** for a comprehensive overview of your assessment options.

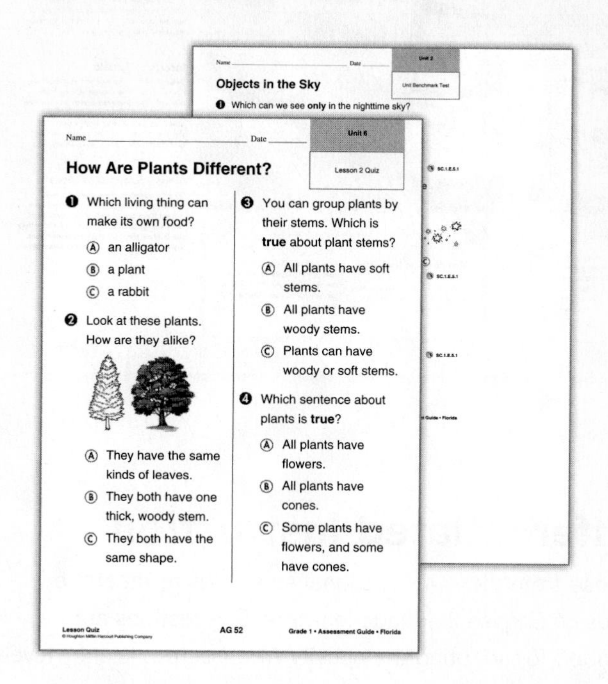

Objects in the Sky

Unit 2 Unit Benchmark Test

1 Which can we see only in the nighttime sky?

Name ____ Date ____

Unit 6 Lesson 2 Quiz

How Are Plants Different?

1 Which living thing can make its own food?

(A) an alligator
(B) a plant
(C) a rabbit

2 Look at these plants. How are they alike?

(A) They have the same kinds of leaves.
(B) They both have one thick, woody stem.
(C) They both have the same shape.

3 You can group plants by their stems. Which is **true** about plant stems?

(A) All plants have soft stems.
(B) All plants have woody stems.
(C) Plants can have woody or soft stems.

4 Which sentence about plants is **true**?

(A) All plants have flowers.
(B) All plants have cones.
(C) Some plants have flowers, and some have cones.

Lesson Quiz AG 52 Grade 1 • Assessment Guide • Florida

Teacher Online Management Center

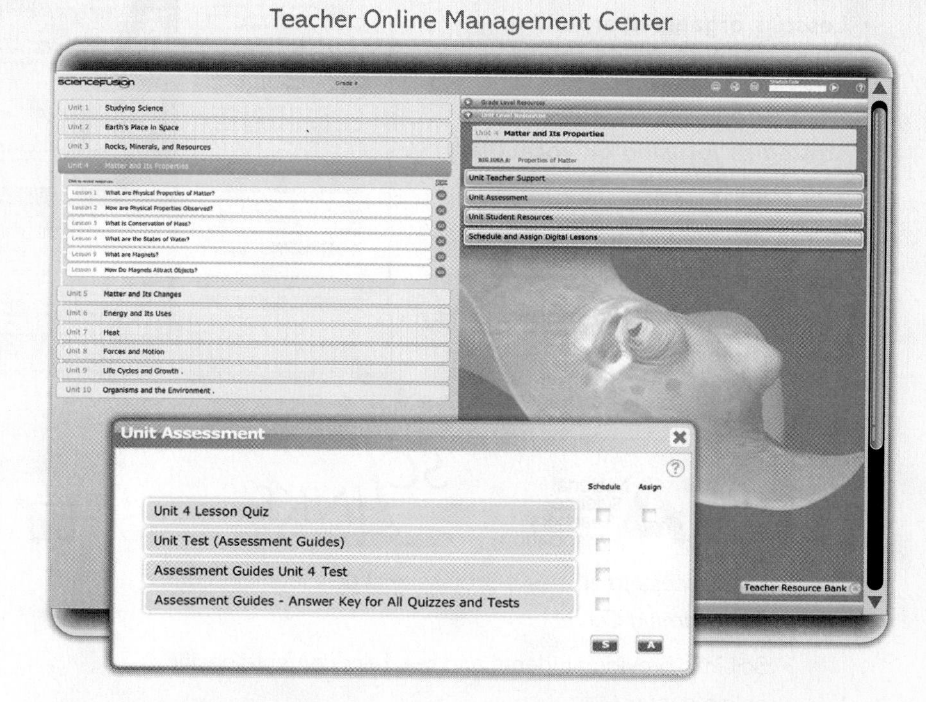

Print Assessment

The print **Assessment Guide** includes

- **Lesson Quizzes**
- **Unit Tests**
- **Unit Performance Assessments**

Online Assessment

The **Digital Assessment** includes

- **assignable leveled assessments for individuals**
- **customizable lesson quizzes and unit tests**
- **individual and whole class reporting**

Customizing Assessment for Your Classroom

Editable quizzes and tests are available in ExamView and online at **thinkcentral.com.** You can customize a quiz or test by adding or deleting items, revising difficulty levels, changing formats, revising sequence, and editing items. Students can also take quizzes and tests directly online.

Choose Your Options

with two powerful teaching tools—a comprehensive **Teacher Edition** and the **Teacher Online Management Center.**

Print

Classroom Management Teacher Edition

Each lesson has a wealth of teaching support, including activities, probing questions, misconception alerts, differentiated instruction, and vocabulary support.

- **Lessons organized around a 5E lesson format**
- **Science Notebooking strategies focusing on vocabulary and inquiry**
- **Strategies for helping young science students build and develop science concepts and inquiry skills for every lesson**

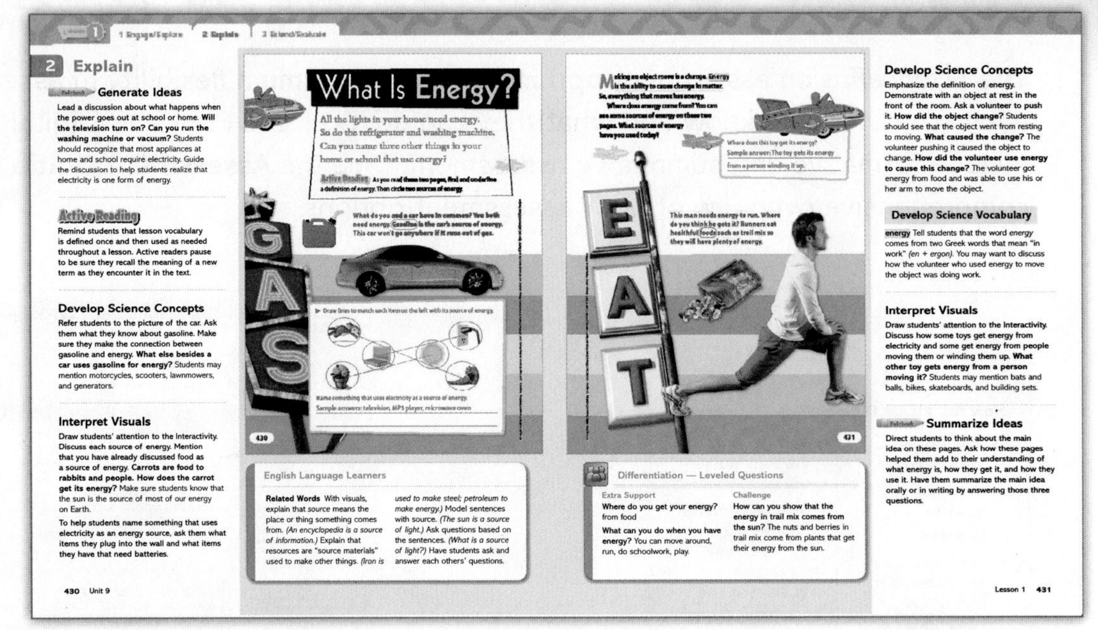

1 Engage/Explore 2 Explain 3 Extend/Evaluate

2 Explain

Generate Ideas

Lead a discussion about what happens when the power goes out at school or home. **Will the television turn on? Can you run the washing machine or vacuum?** Students should recognize that most appliances at home and school require electricity. Guide the discussion to help students realize that electricity is one form of energy.

Active Reading

Remind students that lesson vocabulary is defined once and then used as needed throughout a lesson. Active readers pause to be sure they recall the meaning of a new term as they encounter it in the text.

Develop Science Concepts

Refer students to the picture of the car. Ask them what they know about gasoline. Make sure they make the connection between gasoline and energy. **What else besides a car uses gasoline for energy?** Students may mention motorcycles, scooters, lawnmowers, and generators.

Interpret Visuals

Draw students' attention to the Interactivity. Discuss each source of energy. Mention that you have already discussed food as a source of energy. **Carrots are food to rabbits and people. How does the carrot get its energy?** Make sure students know that the sun is the source of most of our energy on Earth.

To help students name something that uses electricity as an energy source, ask them what items they plug into the wall and what items they have that need batteries.

430 Unit 9

English Language Learners

Related Words With visuals, explain that *source* means the place or thing something comes from. *(An encyclopedia is a source of information.)* Explain that resources are "source materials" used to make other things. *(Iron is used to make steel; petroleum to make energy.)* Model sentences with source. *(The sun is a source of light.)* Ask questions based on the sentences. *(What is a source of light?)* Have students ask and answer each others' questions.

Differentiation — Leveled Questions

Extra Support

Where do you get your energy? from food

What can you do when you have energy? You can move around, run, do schoolwork, play.

Challenge

How can you show that the energy in trail mix comes from the sun? The nuts and berries in trail mix come from plants that get their energy from the sun.

Develop Science Concepts

Emphasize the definition of energy. Demonstrate with an object at rest in the front of the room. Ask a volunteer to push it. **How did the object change?** Students should see that the object went from resting to moving. **What caused the change?** The volunteer pushing it caused the object to change. **How did the volunteer use energy to cause this change?** The volunteer got energy from food and was able to use his or her arm to move the object.

Develop Science Vocabulary

energy Tell students that the word *energy* comes from two Greek words that mean "in work" *(en + ergon)*. You may want to discuss how the volunteer who used energy to move the object was doing work.

Interpret Visuals

Draw students' attention to the Interactivity. Discuss how some toys get energy from electricity and some get energy from people moving them or winding them up. **What other toy gets energy from a person moving it?** Students may mention bats and balls, bikes, skateboards, and building sets.

Summarize Ideas

Direct students to think about the main idea on these pages. Ask how these pages helped them add to their understanding of what energy is, how they get it, and how they use it. Have them summarize the main idea orally or in writing by answering those three questions.

Lesson 1 431

- Easy access to NSTA's e-professional development center, *The Learning Center*
- SciLinks provide students and teachers content-specific online support.

RTI Response to Intervention

Response to Intervention is a process for identifying and supporting students who are not making expected progress toward essential learning goals.

Professional Development

Unit and lesson level professional development focuses on supporting teachers and building educator capacity in key areas of academic achievement.

Differentiated Instruction

Choose from these instructional strategies to meet the needs of English language learners. Suggestions are provided for adapting the activity for three proficiency levels.

Enduring Understandings

Use the suggestions from this section to help students revisit lesson Essential Questions and develop mastery for the Unit Big Idea.

Planning for Inquiry

Preview Inquiry Activities and Lessons to gather and manage the materials needed for each lesson.

Classroom Management
Online teaching and planning

ScienceFusion is a comprehensive, multimodal science program that provides all the digital tools teachers need to engage students in inquiry-based learning. *The Teacher Online Management Center,* at thinkcentral.com, is designed to make it easier for teachers to access program resources to plan, teach, assess, and track.

- Program resources can be easily previewed in PDF format and downloaded for editing.
- Assign and schedule resources online, and they will appear in your students' inboxes.
- All quizzes and tests can be taken and automatically scored online.
- Easily monitor and track student progress.

Teaching with Technology Made Easy

ScienceFusion's 3,000+ animations, simulations, videos, & interactivities are organized to provide:

- flexible options for delivering exciting and engaging digital lessons;
- Teacher Resource Questions, for every lesson, ensure the important information is learned;
- multimodal learning options that connect online learning to concepts learned from reading, writing, and hands-on inquiry.

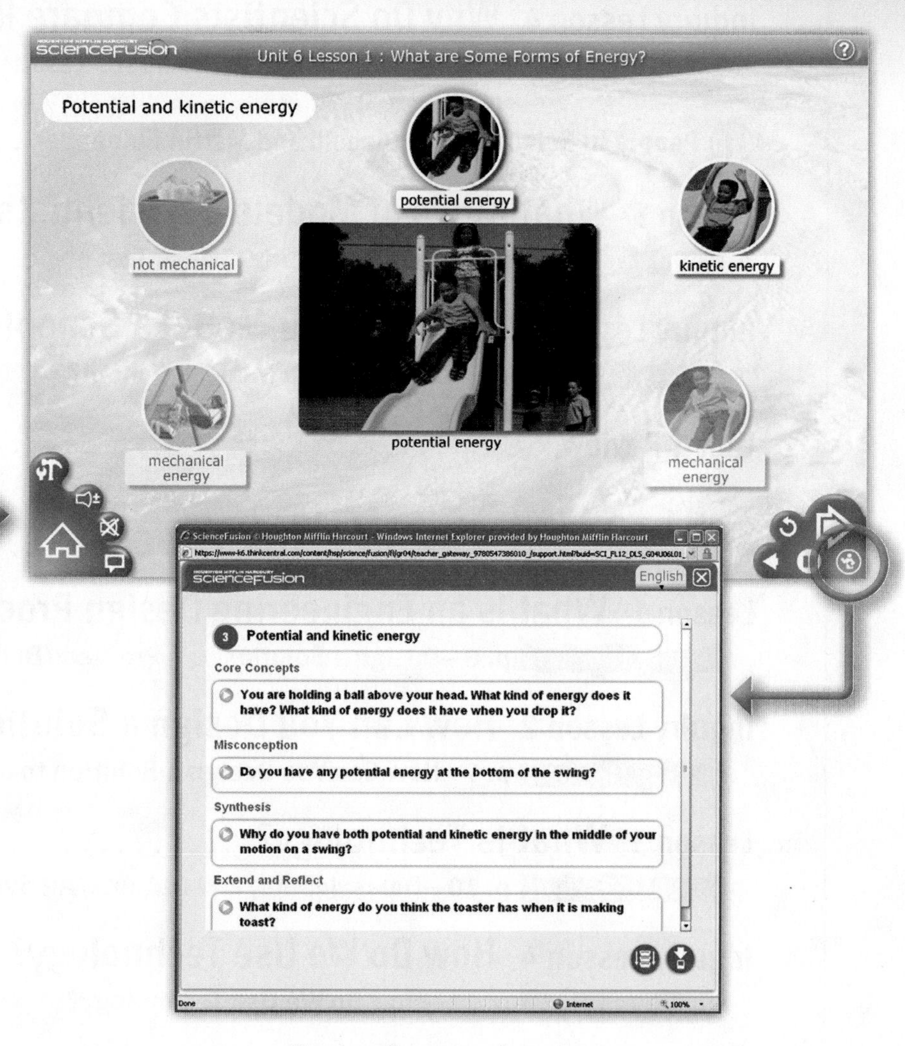

Teacher Resource Questions

Student Edition Contents

Levels of Inquiry Key ■ DIRECTED ■ GUIDED ■ INDEPENDENT

THE NATURE OF SCIENCE AND S.T.E.M.

LIFE SCIENCE

PHYSICAL SCIENCE

ScienceFusion

Video-Based Projects

 **Available in Online Resources**

This video series, hosted by program authors Michael Heithaus and Michael DiSpezio, develops science learning through real-world science and engineering challenges.

Ecology

Leave your lab coat at home! Not all science research takes place in a lab. Host Michael Heithaus takes you around the globe to see ecology field research, including tagging sharks and tracking sea turtles. Students research, graph, and analyze results to complete the project worksheets.

Grade	Video Title
3	Exploring the Galápagos Islands Tent-Making Bats
4	Alligators Up Close Rainforest Habitats
5	The Sea Turtles of Shark Bay

S.T.E.M. Science, Technology, Engineering, and Math

Host Michael DiSpezio poses a series of design problems that challenge students' ingenuity. Each video follows the engineering design process. Worksheets guide students through the process and help them document their results.

Grade	Video Title
3	Take It to Great Heights
4	It's a Bird! It's a Plane!
5	No Gas Needed Get Focused! A Cut Above **

** In Partnership with Children's Hospital Boston

Designed for Grades 3-5, the videos may also be viewed by primary-grade classes if appropriate.

ScienceFusion

Program Scope and Sequence

ScienceFusion is organized by five major strands of science. Each strand includes Big Ideas that flow throughout all grade levels and build in rigor as students move to higher grades.

ScienceFusion Grade Levels and Units

	GRADE K	GRADE 1	GRADE 2	GRADE 3
Nature of Science	**Unit 1** Doing Science	**Unit 1** How Scientists Work	**Unit 1** Work Like a Scientist	**Unit 1** Investigating Questions
STEM		**Unit 2** Technology All Around Us	**Unit 2** Technology and Our World	**Unit 2** The Engineering Process
Life Science	**Unit 2** Animals **Unit 3** Plants **Unit 4** Habitats	**Unit 3** Animals **Unit 4** Plants **Unit 5** Environments	**Unit 3** All About Animals **Unit 4** All About Plants **Unit 5** Environments for Living Things	**Unit 3** Plants and Animals **Unit 4** Ecosystems and Interactions

GRADE 4	GRADE 5	GRADES 6-8
Unit 1 Studying Science	**Unit 1** How Scientists Work	**Module K** Introduction to Science and Technology **Unit 1** The Nature of Science **Unit 2** Measurement and Data
Unit 2 The Engineering Process	**Unit 2** The Engineering Process	**Module K** Introduction to Science and Technology **Unit 3** Engineering, Technology, and Society
Unit 3 Plants and Animals **Unit 4** Energy and Ecosystems	**Unit 3** Cells to Body Systems **Unit 4** Living Things Grow and Reproduce **Unit 5** Ecosystems **Unit 6** Energy and Ecosystems **Unit 7** Natural Resources	**Module A** Cells and Heredity **Unit 1** Cells **Unit 2** Reproduction and Heredity **Module B** The Diversity of Living Things **Unit 1** Life over Time **Unit 2** Earth's Organisms **Module C** The Human Body **Unit 1** Human Body Systems **Unit 2** Human Health **Module D** Ecology and the Environment **Unit 1** Interactions of Living Things **Unit 2** Earth's Biomes and Ecosystems **Unit 3** Earth's Resources **Unit 4** Human Impact on the Environment

ScienceFusion Grade Levels and Units

	GRADE K	GRADE 1	GRADE 2	GRADE 3
Earth Science	**Unit 5** Day and Night **Unit 6** Earth's Resources **Unit 7** Weather and the Seasons	**Unit 6** Earth's Resources **Unit 7** Weather and Seasons **Unit 8** Objects in the Sky	**Unit 6** Earth and Its Resources **Unit 7** All About Weather **Unit 8** The Solar System	**Unit 5** Changes to Earth's Surface **Unit 6** People and Resources **Unit 7** Water and Weather **Unit 8** Earth and Its Moon
Physical Science	**Unit 8** Matter **Unit 9** Energy **Unit 10** Motion	**Unit 9** All About Matter **Unit 10** Forces and Energy	**Unit 9** Changes in Matter **Unit 10** Energy and Magnets	**Unit 9** Matter **Unit 10** Simple and Compound Machines

GRADE 4	GRADE 5	GRADES 6-8
Unit 5 Weather **Unit 6** Earth and Space	**Unit 8** Changes to Earth's Surface **Unit 9** The Rock Cycle **Unit 10** Fossils **Unit 11** Earth's Oceans **Unit 12** The Solar System and the Universe	**Module E** The Dynamic Earth **Unit 1** Earth's Surface **Unit 2** Earth's History **Unit 3** Minerals and Rocks **Unit 4** The Restless Earth **Module F** Earth's Water and Atmosphere **Unit 1** Earth's Water **Unit 2** Oceanography **Unit 3** Earth's Atmosphere **Unit 4** Weather and Climate **Module G** Space Science **Unit 1** The Universe **Unit 2** The Solar System **Unit 3** The Earth-Moon-Sun System **Unit 4** Exploring Space
Unit 7 Properties of Matter **Unit 8** Changes in Matter **Unit 9** Energy **Unit 10** Electricity **Unit 11** Motion	**Unit 13** Matter **Unit 14** Light and Sound **Unit 15** Forces and Motion	**Module H** Matter and Energy **Unit 1** Matter **Unit 2** Energy **Unit 3** Atoms and the Periodic Table **Unit 4** Interactions of Matter **Unit 5** Solutions, Acids, and Bases **Module I** Motion, Forces, and Energy **Unit 1** Motion and Forces **Unit 2** Work, Energy, and Machines **Unit 3** Electricity and Magnetism **Module J** Sound and Light **Unit 1** Introduction to Waves **Unit 2** Sound **Unit 3** Light

Program Pacing

The following pacing guide recommends days for the core print and digital instructional elements of each unit. Additional days can be added for optional inquiry, activities, and extensions.

DAYS	NATURE OF SCIENCE S.T.E.M.
Unit 1 Studying Science	
9	Print or Digital Lesson Content
4	Inquiry Lesson or Virtual Lab
1	Unit Review and Assessment
Unit 2 The Engineering Process	
5	Print or Digital Lesson Content
4	Inquiry Lesson or Virtual Lab
1	Unit Review and Assessment
24 DAYS	

DAYS	LIFE SCIENCE
Unit 3 Plants and Animals	
9	Print or Digital Lesson Content
4	Inquiry Lesson or Virtual Lab
2	S.T.E.M. /Engineering and Technology
1	Unit Review and Assessment
Unit 4 Energy and Ecosystems	
9	Print or Digital Lesson Content
4	Inquiry Lesson or Virtual Lab
2	S.T.E.M. /Engineering and Technology
1	Unit Review and Assessment
32 DAYS	

DAYS	EARTH SCIENCE
Unit 5 Weather	
7	Print or Digital Lesson Content
2	Inquiry Lesson or Virtual Lab
2	S.T.E.M. /Engineering and Technology
1	Unit Review and Assessment

DAYS	EARTH SCIENCE (continued)
Unit 6 Earth and Space	
7	Print or Digital Lesson Content
4	Inquiry Lesson or Virtual Lab
2	S.T.E.M. /Engineering and Technology
1	Unit Review and Assessment
26 DAYS	

DAYS	PHYSICAL SCIENCE
Unit 7 Properties of Matter	
5	Print or Digital Lesson Content
4	Inquiry Lesson or Virtual Lab
2	S.T.E.M. /Engineering and Technology
1	Unit Review and Assessment
Unit 8 Changes in Matter	
5	Print or Digital Lesson Content
4	Inquiry Lesson or Virtual Lab
2	S.T.E.M. /Engineering and Technology
1	Unit Review and Assessment
Unit 9 Energy	
7	Print or Digital Lesson Content
6	Inquiry Lesson or Virtual Lab
2	S.T.E.M. /Engineering and Technology
1	Unit Review and Assessment

DAYS	PHYSICAL SCIENCE (continued)
Unit 10 Electricity	
7	Print or Digital Lesson Content
4	Inquiry Lesson or Virtual Lab
2	S.T.E.M. /Engineering and Technology
1	Unit Review and Assessment
Unit 11 Motion	
3	Print or Digital Lesson Content
2	Inquiry Lesson or Virtual Lab
2	S.T.E.M. /Engineering and Technology
1	Unit Review and Assessment
62 DAYS	

Professional Development

Enduring Understandings

Big Ideas, Essential Questions

by Marjorie Frank

It goes without saying that a primary goal for your students is to develop understandings of science concepts that endure well past the next test. The question is, what is the best way to achieve that goal?

Research and learning experts suggest that students learn most effectively through a constructivist approach in which they build concepts through active involvement in their own learning. While constructivism may lead to superior learning on a lesson-by-lesson basis, the approach does not address how to organize lessons into a program of instruction. Schema theory, from cognitive science, suggests that knowledge is organized into units and that information is stored in these units, much as files are stored in a digital or paper folder. Informed by our understanding of schema theory, we set about organizing *ScienceFusion.* We began by identifying the Big Ideas of science.

...eas are generalizations—broad, powerful concepts that connect facts and ...t may otherwise seem unrelated. Big Ideas are implicit understandings that ...orld make sense. Big Ideas define the "folders," or units, of *ScienceFusion.* ...tatement that articulates the overarching teaching and learning goals of

... Questions define the "files," or information, in a unit. Each ...stion identifies the conceptual focus of a lesson that contributes to ... growing understanding of the associated Big Idea. As such, Essential ... your students a sense of direction and purpose.

...*on,* our goal is to provide you with a tool that helps you help your ... Enduring Understandings in science. Our strategy for achieving ... to provide lesson plans with 5E-based learning experiences ...ework informed by schema theory.

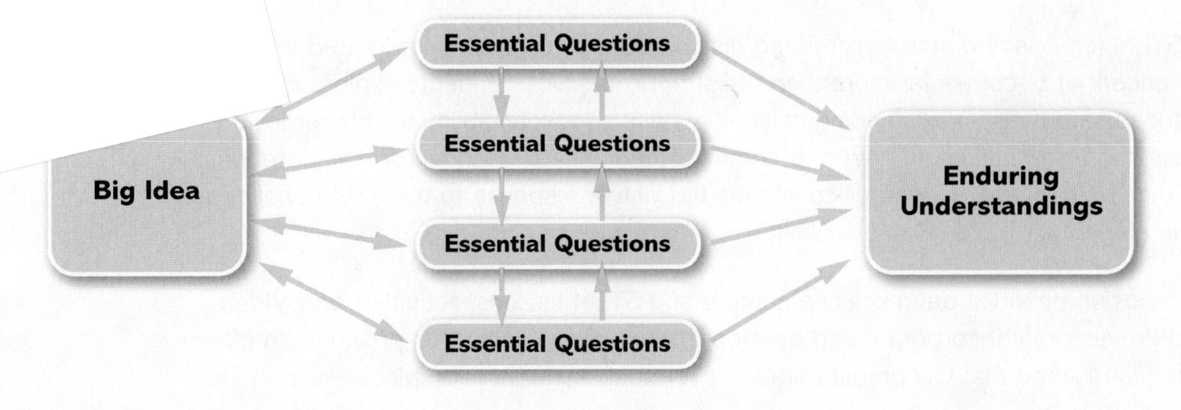

21st Century Skills/STEM

Skills Redefined

by Michael A. DiSpezio

Our world has changed. Globalization and the digital revolution have redefined the skill set that is essential for student success in the classroom and beyond. Known collectively as 21st Century Skills, these areas of competence and aptitude go beyond the three Rs of reading, writing, and arithmetic. 21st Century Skills incorporate a battery of high-level thinking skills and technological capabilities.

21st Century SKILLS A Sample List

Learning and Innovation Skills
- Creativity and Innovation
- Critical Thinking and Problem Solving
- Communication and Collaboration

Information, Media, and Technology Skills
- Information Literacy
- Media Literacy
- ICT (Information, Communications, and Technology) Literacy

Life and Career Skills
- Flexibility and Adaptability
- Initiative and Self-Direction
- Productivity and Accountability
- Leadership and Responsibility

S.T.E.M.

Curriculum that integrates Science, Technology, Engineering, and Mathematics

21st Century Skills are best taught in the context of the core subject areas. Science makes an ideal subject for integrating these important skills because it involves many skills, including inquiry, collaboration, and problem solving. An even deeper level of incorporating these skills can be found with Science, Technology, Engineering, and Mathematics (STEM) lessons and activities. Hands-on STEM lessons that provide students with engineering design challenges are ideal for developing Learning and Innovation Skills. Students develop creativity and innovation as they engineer novel solutions to posed problems. They communicate and collaborate as they engage higher-level thinking skills to help shape their inquiry experience. Students assume ownership of the learning. From this emerges increased self-motivation and personal accountability.

With STEM lessons and activities, related disciplines are seamlessly integrated into a rich experience that becomes far more than the sum of its parts. Students explore real-world scenarios using their understanding of core science concepts, ability for higher level analysis, technological know-how, and communication skills essential for collaboration. From this experience, the learner constructs not only a response to the STEM challenge, but the elements of 21st Century Skills.

ScienceFusion provides deep science content and STEM lessons, activities, and Video-Based Projects that incorporate and develop 21st Century Skills. This provides an effective learning landscape that will prepare students for success in the workplace—and in life.

Professional Development

Differentiated Instruction

Skills Redefined

by Marjorie Frank

Your students learn in different ways, at different speeds, and through different means. Channeling the energy and richness of that diversity is part of the beauty of teaching. A classroom atmosphere that encourages academic risk-taking encourages learning. This is especially true in science, where learning involves making predictions (which could turn out to be inaccurate), offering explanations (which could turn out to be incomplete), and doing things (which could result in observable mistakes).

Like most people, students are more likely to take risks in a low-stress environment where they feel accepted and respected. Science, with its emphasis on exploring through hands-on activities and interactive reading, provides a natural vehicle for low-stress learning. Low stress, however, may mean different things to different people. For students with learning challenges, low stress may mean being encouraged to respond at the level they are able. Another factor in meeting the needs of diverse students is the instructional tools. Are they flexible? Inviting? *ScienceFusion* addresses the needs of diverse students at every step in the instructional process.

As You Plan

Select from these resources to meet individual needs.

- The planning pages at the beginning of each unit in the Teacher Editions identify resources and strategies geared to diverse learners.
- Online Resource: Digital lessons and virtual labs appeal to all students, especially struggling readers and visual learners. Extra Support for Vocabulary and Concepts are reproducible pages for use with struggling readers and students who need additional reinforcement.
- Student Edition with Audio for use with students who have vision impairments or learning difficulties.
- Leveled Readers reinforce, enrich, and extend concepts. A Teacher Guide for each Reader provides instructional strategies and includes reproducible worksheets for Vocabulary, Comprehension, and Oral Reading Fluency.

As You Teach

Take advantage of these point-of-use features.

- A mix of Directed Inquiries and Independent Inquiries suitable for different kinds of learners
- Interactive digital lessons
- Leveled questions for Extra Support, Enrichment, and English Language Learners
- Make Connections: Easy, Average, and Challenging follow-up activities.

As You Reach Out to Families

Look for these school-home connections.

- Take It Home! at the end of every lesson in the Student Edition and Teacher's Edition
- Customizable School-Home Connection Letters for every lesson, available online.

Professional Development

The 5E Model and Levels of Inquiry

by
Michael A. DiSpezio

How do students best learn science? Extensive research and data show that the most effective learning emerges from situations in which one builds understanding based upon personal experiences. Learning is not transmitted from instructor to passive receiver; instead, understanding is constructed through the experience.

The 5E Model for Effective Science Lessons

In the 1960s, Robert Karplus and his colleagues developed a three-step instructional model that became known as the Learning Cycle. This model was expanded into what is today referred to as the 5E Model. To emulate the elements of how an actual scientist works, this model is broken down into five components for an effective lesson: Engage, Explore, Explain, Extend (or Elaborate), and Evaluate.

Engage—The engagement sets the scene for learning. It is a warm-up during which students are introduced to the learning experience. Prior knowledge is assessed and its analysis used to develop an effective plan to meet stated objectives. Typically, an essential question is then posed; the question leads the now motivated and engaged students into the exploration.

Explore—This is the stage where the students become actively involved in hands-on process. They communicate and collaborate to develop a strategy that addresses the posed problem. Emphasis is placed on inquiry and hands-on investigation. The hands-on experience may be highly prescribed or open-ended in nature.

Explain—Students answer the initial question by using their findings and information they may be reading about, discussing with classmates, or experiencing through digital media. Their experience and understanding of concepts, processes, and hands-on skills is strengthened at this point. New vocabulary may be introduced.

Extend (or Elaborate)—The explanation is now extended to other situations, questions, or problems. During this stage the learner more closely examines findings in terms of context and transferable application. In short, extension reveals the application and implication of the internalized explanation. Extension may involve connections to other curriculum areas.

Evaluate—Although evaluation is an ongoing process, this is the stage in which a final assessment is most often performed. The instructor evaluates lesson effectiveness by using a variety of formal and informal assessment tools to measure student performance.

The 5E lesson format is used in all the *ScienceFusion* Teacher Edition lessons.

Directed, Guided, and Independent Inquiry

It wasn't that long ago that science was taught mostly through demonstration and lecture. Today, however, most instructional strategies integrate an inquiry-based approach to learning science. This methodology is founded in higher-level thinking and facilitates the students' construction of understanding from experience. When offered opportunities to ask questions, design investigations, collect and analyze data, and communicate their findings, each student assumes the role of an active participant in shaping his or her own learning process.

The degree to which any activity engages the inquiry process is variable, from highly prescribed steps to a completely learner-generated design. Researchers have established three distinct levels of inquiry: directed (or structured) inquiry, guided inquiry, and independent (or open) inquiry. These levels are distinguished by the amount of guidance offered by the instructor.

Directed Inquiry In this level of inquiry, the instructor poses a question or suggests an investigation, and students follow a prescribed set of instructions. The outcome may be unknown to the students, but it is known to the instructor. Students follow the structured outline to uncover an outcome that supports the construction of lesson concepts.

Guided Inquiry As in Directed Inquiry, the instructor poses to the students a question to investigate. While students are conducting the investigation, the instruction focuses on developing one or more inquiry skills. Focus may also be provided for students to learn to use methods or tools of science. In *ScienceFusion*, the Teacher Edition provides scaffolding for developing inquiry skills, science methods, or tools. Student pages accompany these lessons and provide prompts for writing hypotheses, recording data, and drawing conclusions.

Independent Inquiry This is the most complex level of inquiry experience. A prompt is provided, but students must design their own investigation in response to the prompt. In some cases, students will write their own questions and then plan and perform scientific investigations that will answer those questions. This level of inquiry is often used for science fair projects. Independent Inquiry does not necessarily mean individual inquiry. Investigations can be conducted by individual students or by pairs or teams of students.

Response to Intervention

by Marjorie Frank

In a traditional model, assessment marks the end of an instructional cycle. Students work through a unit, take a test, and move on, regardless of their performance. However, current research suggests that assessment should be part of the instructional cycle, that it should be ongoing, and that it should be used to identify students needing intervention. This may sound like a tall order—who wants to give tests all the time?—but it may not be as difficult as it seems. In some ways, you are probably doing it already.

Assessment

Every student interaction has the potential to be an assessment. It all depends on how you perceive and use the interaction.

- Suppose you ask a question. You can just listen to your student's response, or you can assess it. Does the response indicate comprehension of the concept? If not, intervention may be needed.
- Suppose a student offers an explanation of a phenomenon depicted in a photo. You can assess the explanation. Does it show accurate factual knowledge? Does it reveal a misconception? If so, intervention may be needed.
- Suppose a student draws a diagram to illustrate a concept. You can assess the diagram. Is it accurate? If not, intervention may be needed.

As the examples indicate, assessing students' understandings can—and should—be an integral part of the instructional cycle and be used to make decisions about the next steps of instruction. For students making good progress, next steps might be exploring a related concept, a new lesson, or an additional challenge. For students who are not making adequate progress, intervention may be needed.

Assessment and intervention are tightly linked. Assessment leads to intervention—fresh approaches, different groupings, new materials—which, in turn, leads to assessment. Response to Intervention (RTI) gives shape and substance to this linkage.

RTI Response to Intervention

Response to Intervention is a process for identifying and supporting students who are not making expected progress toward essential learning goals.

RTI is a three-tiered approach based on an ongoing cycle of superior instruction, frequent monitoring of students' learning (assessments), and appropriate interventions. Students who are found not to be making expected progress in one Tier move to the next higher Tier, where they receive more intense instruction.

- **Tier I:** Students receive whole-class, core instruction.
- **Tier II:** Students work in small groups that supplement and reinforce core instruction.
- **Tier III:** Students receive individualized instruction.

How RTI and *ScienceFusion* Work

ScienceFusion provides many opportunities to assess students' understanding and many components appropriate for students in all Tiers.

TIER III Intensive Intervention

Individualized instruction, with options for auditory, visual, and second language learners. Special education is a possibility.

Online Student Edition

ScienceFusion Components

Online Student Edition lessons with audio recordings	**Appropriate for:** • Auditory learners
Online Extra Support for Vocabulary and Concepts	**Appropriate for:** • Struggling readers • Second-language learners

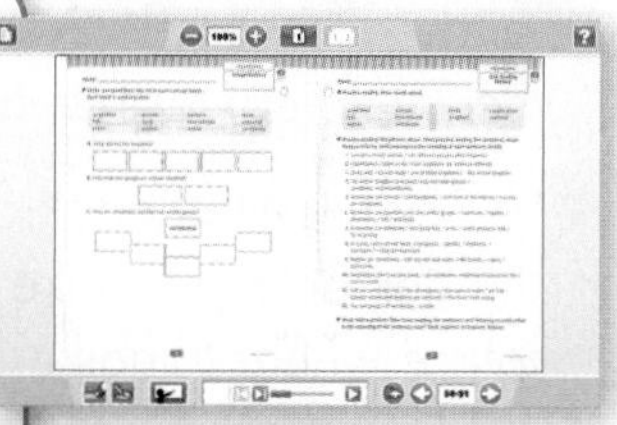

Extra Support

Students achieving at a lower level than their peers in Tier II

TIER II Strategic Intervention

Small Group Instruction in addition to core instruction

Worksheets

ScienceFusion Components

Vocabulary Worksheets
Comprehension Worksheets
Oral Reading Fluency Worksheet

Below-Level Reader
Teacher Guide for Below-Level Reader

Appropriate for:
- Struggling readers
- Visual learners
- Second-language learners
- Screening tools to assess students' responses to Tier II instruction

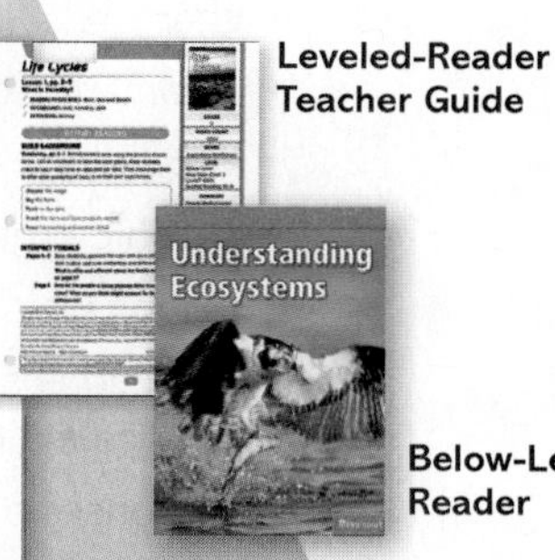

Leveled-Reader Teacher Guide

Below-Level Reader

Students achieving at a lower level than their peers in Tier I

TIER I Core Classroom Instruction

With the help of extensive point-of-use strategies that support superior teaching, students receive whole-class instruction and engage productively in small-group work as appropriate.

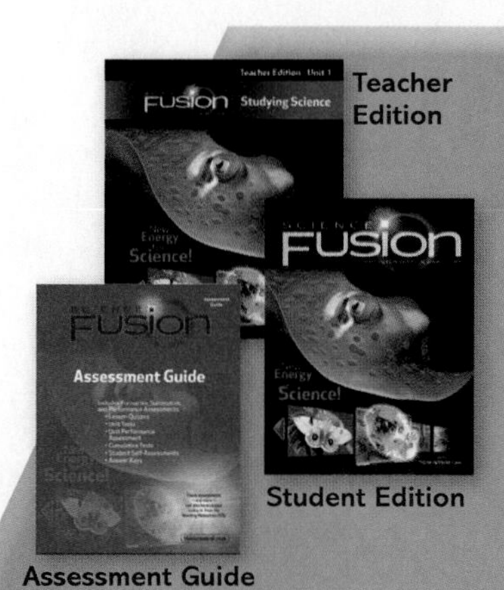

Teacher Edition

Student Edition

Assessment Guide

ScienceFusion Components

Student Edition
Teacher Edition
Assessment Guide
Online Digital Curriculum

Appropriate for:
- Screening tools to access students' responses to Tier I instruction
- Tier I intervention for students unable to complete the activity independently

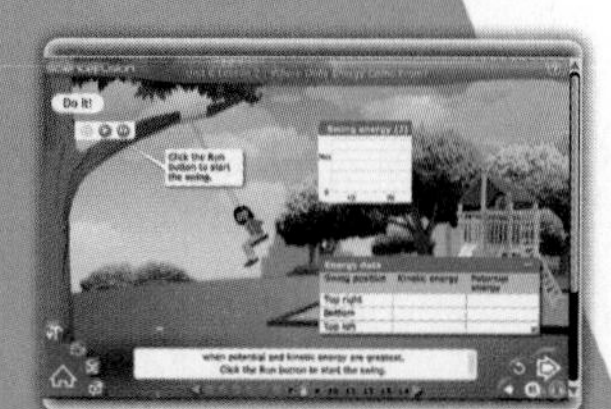

Digital Curriculum

Professional Development

Science Notebooks

The What, Why, Who, When, Where and How!

Science Notebooks are powerful tools, and they play an important role in every teacher's in box. They lead your students deep into the learning process, and they provide you with a window into that process as well as a means to communicate about it.

by Marjorie Frank

What Are Science Notebooks?

A notebook contains the writer's ideas, observations, and perceptions of events and endeavors. A Science Notebook contains ideas about and observations of scientific processes, data, conclusions, conjectures, and generalizations.

A Science Notebook can be in many formats--spiral bound, tablet, loose pages in a binder, or digital. Like an ordinary notebook, it functions much like a storehouse, a place where things are collected and held. The "things" in a Science Notebook can be just about anything related to what students are doing and learning in science:

- observations and data
- drawings and diagrams of structures and processes
- graphs
- charts
- summaries of new concepts or a textbook lesson
- vocabulary words with definitions and drawings
- graphic organizers showing how ideas are connected
- responses to lessons or a specific learning experience
- reflections about their work and the meaning they derived from science experiences
- responses to questions
- new questions
- predictions and plans for an investigation
- observations and conclusions
- drawings or sketches from field trips
- original stories and poems about science topics
- science applications in daily life

A Science Notebook is especially important when students do inquiry-based or project-based learning. It offers students a single place to record their observations, consider possibilities, and organize their thoughts. As such, it is a learner's version of the logs professional scientists keep.

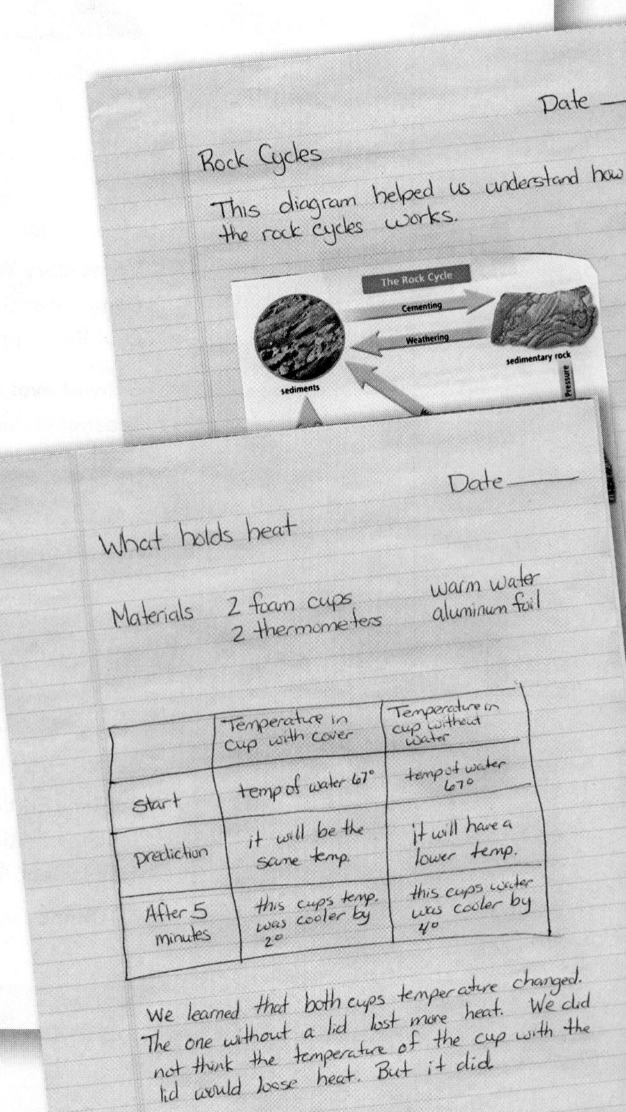

Why Bother with Science Notebooks?

No doubt, it takes time and effort to help students set up and maintain Science Notebooks, not to mention the time it takes you to review them and provide meaningful feedback. The payoff better be worth it, you're probably saying to yourself. And it is. Here's why.

Keeping a Science Notebook:

- leads each learner to engage with ideas (not just those who raise their hands in class)
- engages students in writing–an active, thinking, analytical process
- causes students to organize their thinking
- helps students develop 21st Century organizational skills
- enables students to express themselves creatively
- provides students with multiple opportunities and modes to process new information
- makes learning experiences more personal
- provides students with a record of their own progress and accomplishments
- doubles as a study guide for formal assessments
- creates a vehicle for students to improve their reading and writing skills

Who Should Keep a Science Notebook?

Every single student, regardless of age, aptitude, or language background.

Science Notebooks are well suited for differentiating instruction. By allowing students to draw about their investigations and use the glossary to label their drawings, you can include all students in the process. Students can also work in pairs to do shared writing.

Kindergarten and first grade learners may dictate brief captions to pictures that tell their science story. Or, they may benefit from working as a class to construct a science "big book."

When Should Students Work in Their Science Notebooks?

During every single science class.

On some days, students may only write a summary of a lesson, or write a response to an experience. On other days, they may attach a data sheet they completed during an investigation, or write a longer entry that includes diagrams, data, conclusions, and reflections.

Notebook ▸ Where Should Science Notebooks Be Stored?

In school. The Notebooks can be stored in a basket, in a bin, or behind a colored tab in a file cabinet. If students are working in groups or teams, each team may have its own basket or bin. Use color-coding for easy identification. Store the Notebooks near the science materials if there's space.

Notebook ▸ How Can I Get Started with Science Notebooks in My Class?

You'll want to have students set up their Science Notebooks as soon as possible after school begins, so they can be used throughout the year. If you are new to Notebooking, you might want to follow these steps or modify them to suit your needs.

1. After deciding on a Notebook format–spiral, pad, loose leaf in a binder, or digital — invite students to make a cover. Encourage students to decorate the cover so it can be easily distinguished and to include their names and other appropriate information, such as your name and the class period.
2. Use the first three or four pages to create a Table of Contents. Remind students to write "Table of Contents" at the top of each page.
3. Set up three columns on each Contents page and label the columns *Page, Activity,* and *Dates*.
4. Number the pages. While this may seem like a tedious task, it will pay off many times over during the year.
5. Although *ScienceFusion* has an interactive glossary at the back of the Student Edition, you may want students to use the last ten or twelve pages of their Science Notebooks for a glossary.

Now your students are all set!

For each activity or concept, students should start a new page. After they complete their work, they should return to the Table of Contents and fill in the information.

Keeping Place in the Notebooks

Students can lose valuable time trying to find their place in their Notebook. Here are some ways to get around the problem:

- **Have students use a binder clip to hold all the unused pages. During each lesson, they can remove newly used pages from the clip.**
- **Suggest that students tape a string to the spiral or spine of a binder and place the string between the used and unused pages.**
- **Encourage students to use a sticky-note to mark the last used page or first unused page.**

Notebook How Can I Give My Students Feedback on Their Notebooks?

Giving feedback is one of the most important strategies you can use to support students' learning. You'll want to review your students' Notebooks as often as possible. This is a case where more really is better. Students need to know their Notebooks are important. Regular feedback sends that message.

Many teachers provide critical feedback to coincide with points in the curriculum where mastery is key to moving on–for example, in the middle and at the end of a unit.

- Be sure you have a clear understanding of the lesson objective. This will help you decide how to comment on whether a student has met the objective. In *ScienceFusion*, a full answer to an Essential Question articulates the content of lesson objectives.
- Provide positive feedback directly in a Student's Notebook.
- Make suggestions for additional thought or work on sticky-notes, which can be removed when the work is completed.
- When possible, couch your suggestions as guiding questions such as, What conclusions can you draw from the evidence? Which of the variables will you need to control?

You may wish to have students conduct a self-evaluation of their Science Notebook. This page is available in the *ScienceFusion* Assessment Guide.

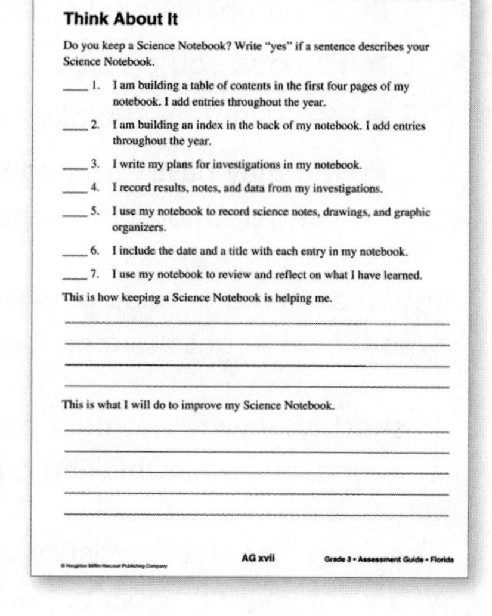
Name ____________

Self Assessment
My Science Notebook

Think About It

Do you keep a Science Notebook? Write "yes" if a sentence describes your Science Notebook.

____ 1. I am building a table of contents in the first four pages of my notebook. I add entries throughout the year.

____ 2. I am building an index in the back of my notebook. I add entries throughout the year.

____ 3. I write my plans for investigations in my notebook.

____ 4. I record results, notes, and data from my investigations.

____ 5. I use my notebook to record science notes, drawings, and graphic organizers.

____ 6. I include the date and a title with each entry in my notebook.

____ 7. I use my notebook to review and reflect on what I have learned.

This is how keeping a Science Notebook is helping me.

This is what I will do to improve my Science Notebook.

© Houghton Mifflin Harcourt Publishing Company AG xvii Grade 3 • Assessment Guide • Florida

Science Notebooks and *ScienceFusion*

Notebook *ScienceFusion* Teacher Editions and the Inquiry Flipcharts include point-of-use suggestions and strategies for Science Notebook entries. Look for the Science Notebook features.

Strategies for using Science Notebooks with all the *ScienceFusion* Inquiry activities are provided in Online Inquiry Support in Online Resources.

Notebook The Teacher Editions also include suggestions for summarizing ideas after each two-page spread. The Science Notebook is an ideal place for students to write their summaries.

As you and your students embrace Notebooking, you will surely find it to be an engaging, enriching, and very valuable endeavor.

Science Notebook

Mixtures Madness

My Planning Questions

Questions	Answers
1. Which three substances will mix together?	
2. Which properties of the substances are important for this investigation?	
3. Which tool or tools will I use to separate the mixture, and why? (related to Question 2)	
4. What other materials will I need?	
5. In what order will I separate the three substances?	

Active Reading

by Marjorie Frank

Reading is a complex process in which readers use their knowledge and experience to make meaning from text. Though rarely accompanied by obvious large-muscle movement, reading is very much an active endeavor.

Think back to your days as a college student when you pored over your textbooks to prepare for class or for an exam—or, more recently, concentrated on an article or book with information you wanted to remember.

- You probably paid close attention to the text.
- Perhaps you paused to ask yourself questions.
- You might have broken off temporarily to look up an important, but unfamiliar, word.
- You may have stopped to reread a challenging passage or to "catch up" if your mind wandered for a moment.

If you owned the reading material, you also may have used a pencil or marker to interact with the text right there on the page (or in a digital file).

In short, you were having a conversation with yourself about the text. You were engaged. You were thinking critically.

These are the characteristics of active readers. This is precisely the kind of reader you want your students to be, because research suggests that active reading enables readers to understand and remember more information.

Active Reading involves interacting with text cognitively, metacognitively, and quite literally. You can actually see active readers at work. They are not sitting quietly as they read; they're underlining, marking, boxing, bracketing, drawing arrows, numbering, and writing comments. Here is what they may be noting:

- key terms and main ideas
- questions they have, opinions, agreements, and disagreements
- important facts and details
- sequences of events
- words, such as *because, before,* and *but,* that signal connections between ideas
- problems/solutions
- definitions and examples

The very process of interacting actively with text helps keep readers focused, thinking, comprehending, and remembering. But interacting in this way means readers are marking up the text. This is exactly why ScienceFusion Student Editions are consumable. They are meant to be marked up.

Active Reading and *ScienceFusion*

ScienceFusion includes Active Reading prompts and strategies on most pages of the Student Editions. The prompts appear at the beginning of each lesson and on most two-page spreads.

The first page of each lesson includes an Active Reading prompt. These prompts give readers a heads-up about the text structure of the lesson—the way the ideas are organized. Reading experts suggest that knowledge of text structure improves comprehension since readers approach the text ready to think about ideas in the same way the writer has organized them. Cause and effect, sequence, compare/contrast, problem/solution, and main idea and details are ways to organize text.

Cause and Effect

Some ideas in this lesson are connected by a cause-and-effect relationship. Why something happens as a result of something else is an effect. Active readers look for effects by asking themselves, What happened? They look for causes by asking, Why did it happen?

Each prompt also includes a specific idea for readers to keep in mind, engaging self-monitoring or metacognitive strategies. This particular prompt gives readers specific questions to ask themselves so they remain focused on causes and effects. Other prompts urge readers to look for specific words that signal a text structure or to preview the text, turning headings into questions the text will answer.

Examples of Active Reading Prompts

- **Draw a star next to the names of animals that hatch from eggs and a check mark next to the names of animals that are born live.**
- **As you read these two pages, circle lesson vocabulary each time it is used.**
- **Find and underline four clues that a chemical change has occured.**
- **Put a *P* next to the sentences that describe a problem. Put an *S* next to the sentences that describe a solution.**

Students' Responses to Active Reading Prompts

Active Reading has benefits for you as well as for your students. You can use students' responses to Active Reading prompts and the other interactive prompts in *ScienceFusion* as ongoing assessments. A quick review of students' responses provides a great deal of information.

- Are students comprehending the text?
- How deeply do they understand the concepts developed?
- Did they get the main idea? the cause? the order in which things happen?

Answers to these questions are available in students' responses to Active Learning prompts throughout a lesson—long before you might see poor results on a test. These frequent and regular assessments are integral parts of an effective Response to Intervention program.

The Active Reading prompts in *ScienceFusion* help make everyone a winner.

Professional Development

Project-Based Learning

For a list of the *ScienceFusion* Video-Based Projects, see page PG21.

by
Michael R. Heithaus

When asked why I decided to become a biologist, the answer is pretty simple. I was inspired by spending almost every day outdoors, exploring under every rock, getting muddy in creeks and streams, and fishing in farm ponds, rivers, and—when I was really lucky—the oceans. Combine that with the spectacular stories of amazing animals and adventures that I saw on TV and I was hooked. As I've progressed in my career as a biologist, that same excitement and curiosity that I had as a ten-year-old looking for a salamander is still driving me.

But today's kids live in a very different world. Cable and satellite TV, Twitter, MP3 players, cell phones, and video games all compete with the outdoors for kids' time and attention. Education budget cuts, legal issues, and the pressures of standardized testing have also limited the opportunities for students to explore outdoors with their teachers.

How do we overcome these challenges so as to inspire kids' curiosity, help them connect with the natural world, and get them to engage in science and math? This is a critical issue. Not only do we need to ensure our national competitiveness and the conservation of our natural resources by training the next generation of scientists, we also need to ensure that every kid grows up to understand how scientists work and why their work is important.

To overcome these challenges, there is no question that we need to grab students' attention and get them to actively engage in the learning process. Research shows that students who are active and engaged participants in their learning have greater gains in concept and skills development than students who are passive in the classroom.

Project-based learning is one way to engage students. And when the stimulus for the project is exciting video content, engaged and active learning is almost guaranteed. Nothing captures a student's attention faster than exciting video. I have noticed that when my university students have video to accompany a lesson, they learn and retain the material better. It's no different for younger students! Videos need to do more than just "talk at" students to have a real impact. Videos need to engage students and require participation.

Teachers and students who use *ScienceFusion* video-based projects have noticed the following:

- The videos use captivating imagery, dynamic scientists, and cool stories to inspire kids to be curious about the world around them.
- Students connect to the projects by having the videos present interesting problems for them to solve.
- The videos engage students with projects woven into the story of the video so students are doing the work of real scientists!

The start-to-finish nature of the video projects, where students do background research and develop their own hypotheses, should lead to students' personal investment in solving the challenges that are presented. By seeing real scientists who are excellent role models gather data that they have to graph and interpret, students will not only learn the science standards being addressed, they will see that they can apply the scientific method to their lives. One day, they too could be a scientist!

Based on my experiences teaching in the university classroom, leading field trips for middle school students, and taking the first project-based videos into the classroom, project-based learning has considerable benefits. The video-based projects generate enthusiasm and curiosity. They also help students develop a deeper understanding of science content as well as how to go about a scientific investigation. If we inspire students to ask questions and seek answers for themselves, we will go a long way toward closing achievement gaps in science and math and facilitate the development of the next generation of scientists and scientifically literate citizens.

Professional Development

Developing Visual Literacy

Science teachers can build the bridges between students' general literacy and their scientific literacy by focusing attention on the particular kinds of reading strategies students need to be successful. One such strategy is that of knowing how to read and interpret the various visual displays used in science.

by
Donna M. Ogle

Many young readers receive little instruction in reading charts, tables, diagrams, photographs, or illustrations in their language arts/reading classes. Science is where these skills can and must be developed. Science provides a meaningful context where students can learn to read visually presented forms of information and to create their own visual representations. Research studies have shown that students take longer to read science materials containing combinations of visual displays and narrative texts than they do to read narrative text alone. The process of reading the combination materials is slower and more difficult because the reader must relate the visual displays to the narrative text and build a meaning that is based on information from both.

We also know that students benefit when teachers take time to explain how each visual form is constructed and to guide students in the thinking needed to make sense of these forms. Even the seemingly simple act of interpreting a photograph needs to be taught to most students. Here are some ways to help students develop the ability to think more critically about what they view:

- Model for students how to look carefully at a photograph and list what they notice.
- Divide the photograph into quadrants and have students think more deeply about what the photographer has used as the focus of the image and what context is provided.
- Have students use language such as *zoom*, *close-up*, *foreground*, *background*, or *panorama views* to describe photographs.

The ability to interpret a photograph is clearly a part of the scientific skill of engaging in careful observation. This skill helps students when they are using print materials, observing nature, and making their own photographs of aspects of their experiments.

Attention to the other forms of visual displays frequently used in science is also important to students' learning of scientific concepts and processes. For example, students in grades 4 through 8 need to learn to interpret and then construct each of the types of graphs, from circle graphs and bar graphs to more complex line graphs.

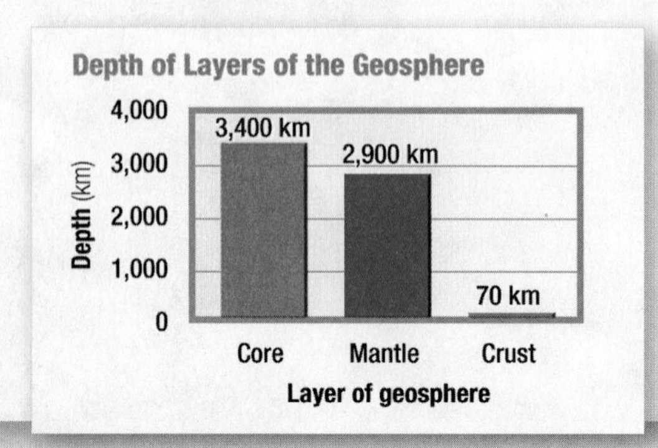

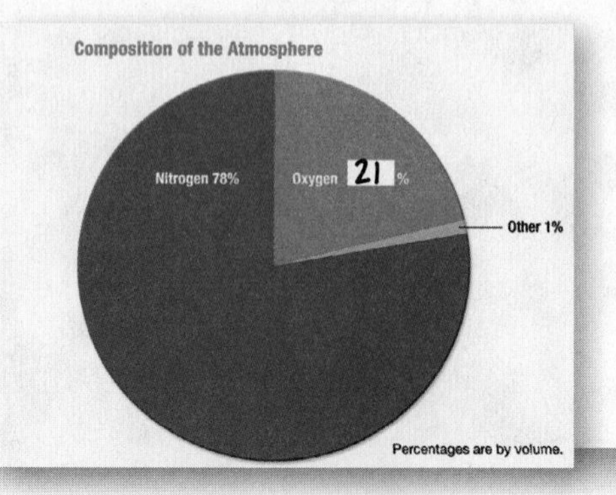

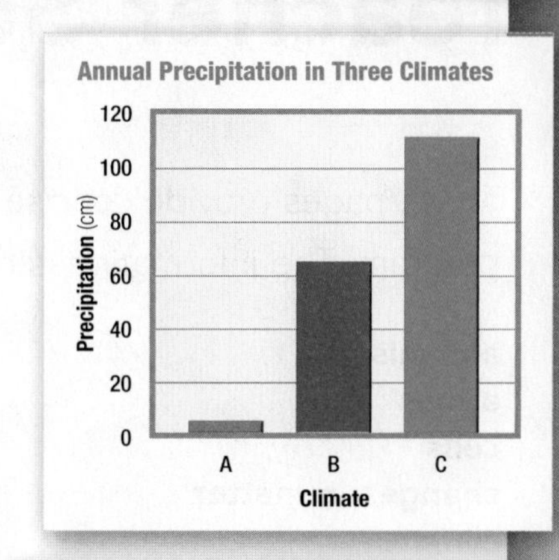

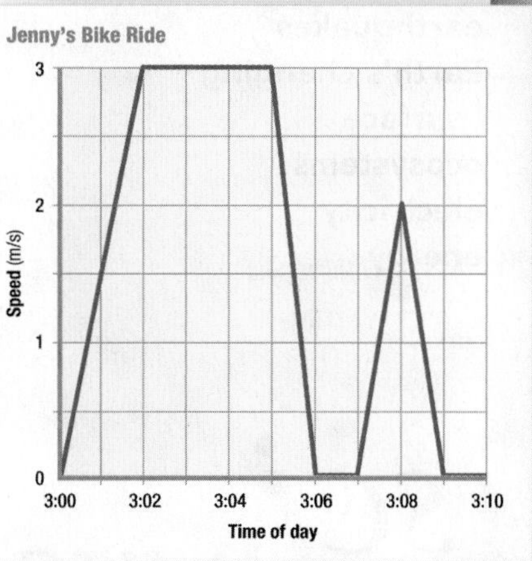

Students also need to be able to read diagrams and flow charts. Yet, in a recent study asking students to think aloud and point to how they visually scan tables and diagrams, we learned how inadequate many students were as readers of these visual forms. Because so much of the scientific information students will encounter is summarized in these visual formats, it is essential that students learn to interpret and construct visual displays.

A second aspect of interpreting visual displays is connecting the information in the visual formats with the narrative text information.
Some students misinterpret what they see in visuals when even a few words differ between the text and the illustration. For example, in this page from a Middle School Student Edition, the text says, "the arm of a human, the front leg of a cat, and the wing of a bat do not look alike . . . but they are similar in structure. "

The diagram labels (lower right) showing the bat wing and the cat's leg use *front limb*, not *wing* or *leg*. For students who struggle with English, the differing terms may cause confusion unless teachers show students how to use clues from later in the paragraph, where limb and wing/arm are connected, and how to connect this information to the two drawings. In some cases teachers have students draw lines showing where visual displays connect with the more extensive narrative text content. Developing students' awareness of how visual and narrative information support each other and yet provide different forms in which information can be shared is an important step in building scientific literacy.

Reading science requires students to use specific reading strategies. The more carefully science teachers across grade levels assess what students already know about reading scientific materials, the more easily they can focus instruction to build the scaffolds students need to gain independence and confidence in their reading and learning of science. Time spent explaining, modeling, and guiding students will yield the rewards of heightened student enjoyment, confidence, and engagement in the exciting world of scientific inquiry.

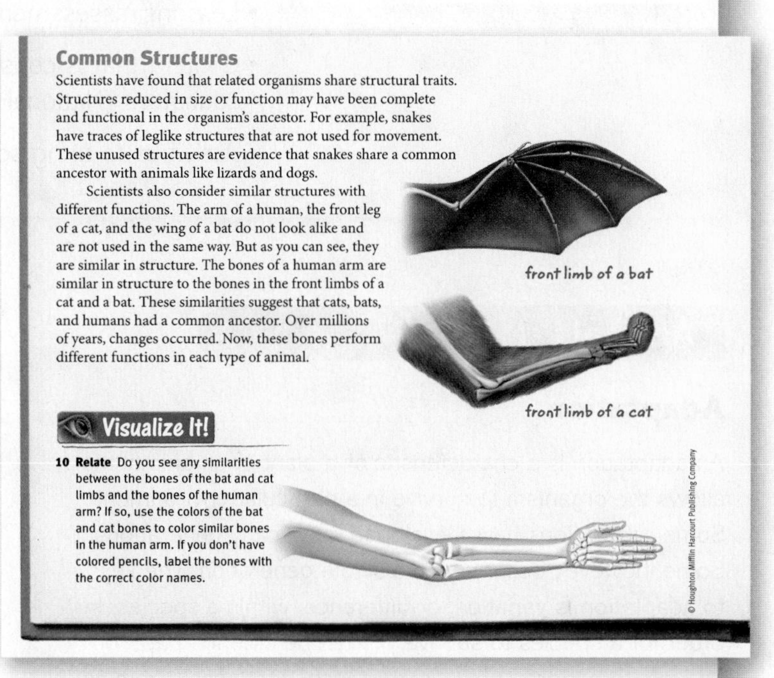
Common Structures

Scientists have found that related organisms share structural traits. Structures reduced in size or function may have been complete and functional in the organism's ancestor. For example, snakes have traces of leglike structures that are not used for movement. These unused structures are evidence that snakes share a common ancestor with animals like lizards and dogs.

Scientists also consider similar structures with different functions. The arm of a human, the front leg of a cat, and the wing of a bat do not look alike and are not used in the same way. But as you can see, they are similar in structure. The bones of a human arm are similar in structure to the bones in the front limbs of a cat and a bat. These similarities suggest that cats, bats, and humans had a common ancestor. Over millions of years, changes occurred. Now, these bones perform different functions in each type of animal.

front limb of a bat

front limb of a cat

Visualize It!

10 Relate Do you see any similarities between the bones of the bat and cat limbs and the bones of the human arm? If so, use the colors of the bat and cat bones to color similar bones in the human arm. If you don't have colored pencils, label the bones with the correct color names.

Teacher Science Background

These pages provide concise science background for the major topics and concepts in this program. The information is organized according to the following key words:

animals
atoms
cells
changes in matter
climate
earthquakes
Earth's changing surface
ecosystems
electricity
energy
engineering and technology
engineering design process
exploring space
food chains and food webs
forces
fossils
heredity
human body
inquiry skills
landforms
light
magnetism
measuring matter
meteorology
minerals
motion
natural resources
oceans
planetary cycles
plants
plate tectonics
properties of matter
rocks
scientific methods
scientific tools
simple machines
solar system
sound
states of matter
volcanoes
water
water cycle

Additional background information is provided in Online Resources. The online content, appropriate for teachers and students, provides the following benefits:

- Free up-to-date web content to extend and expand student understanding
- Lessons, assessments, and deeper exploration of content for teachers
- Content that is constantly reviewed and vetted by experienced NSTA educators (National Science Teachers Association)
- Activities to bring science alive in the classroom

Animals

Adaptation

An adaptation is a characteristic of a plant or an animal that allows the organism to survive in a particular environment. Some adaptations have developed over many generations. Some, however, occur within a single generation. The key to adaptation is variation, or difference, within a species. In order for a species to survive, it must be able to adapt, or change, to better fit new circumstances that arise within an environment. Adaptations can take the form of changes both in an organism's body (physical adaptation) and in its behavior (behavioral adaptation). An example of the former is the long, pointed beak of the hummingbird, which is designed to fit inside tubular flowers. An example of the latter is the nest-building and courting-dance activity of the male bower bird that helps him attract a mate. These adaptations do not happen during one animal's lifetime, but over many generations. The shape of a bird's beak, the placement of a fish's eyes, and the shape of a mammal's teeth are just a few adaptations that help animals survive.

How Animals Are Born and Grow

All animals produce offspring in one of two ways. Some animals hatch from eggs, while others develop inside the mother before she gives birth. Some animals look like their parents when they are born and others do not. Some need a lot of parental care; others need little. All need food, water, air, and shelter to survive. Either the parent helps the young meet these needs, or the young are equipped to meet them. In species where there is little or no parenting, the adults produce many offspring to compensate for those lost to predators. An animal's body covering also changes as the animal grows. Young animals that have to fend for themselves tend to develop mature body coverings faster than animals that receive parental care.

Protective Body Coverings

An animal's body covering protects an animal from the harmful elements of its environment. The hard outer shell of an insect and the sharp quills of a porcupine act as shields around these organisms. Body coverings also protect animals from extreme temperatures. Thick hair traps an animal's body heat to insulate it in a cold environment. Thin porous skin enables an animal to release body heat and keep cool in a warm environment.

Animal Classification

Living things can be grouped into domains and kingdoms. Two of the kingdoms are the plant kingdom and the animal kingdom. To organize the thousands of different species in the animal kingdom, zoologists group animals into categories according to their genetic makeup and their physical similarities and differences. Zoologists divide the animal kingdom into smaller and smaller groups called *subkingdoms*, *phyla*, and *subphyla*. This classification system is called a *taxonomy*. Animals can further be divided into smaller groups. The science of animal classification has been developing for more than 300 years. Because contemporary scientists can study the genetic makeup of animals, scientists can now group them in more ways. They have even found some new groups. Some animals may seem to belong to one group but actually belong to another. For example, a whale lives in water like a fish, but it is a mammal. It feeds milk to its young, and it has lungs instead of gills.

Vertebrates and Invertebrates

The terms *vertebrate* and *invertebrate* are used by scientists as a matter of convenience. The terms do not indicate a natural division in the animal kingdom because the divisions do not indicate the real relationships among the animals in the groups. Some invertebrates are more closely related to the vertebrates than they are to other invertebrates. For example, echinoderms (the group that includes sand dollars, sea stars, and sea urchins) belong to a group of animals called *deuterostomes*. The term describes the animals' embryonic development. All vertebrates are deuterostomes. Most other groups of invertebrates, however, belong to a group called *protostomes*. Thus, echinoderms are inferred to be more closely related to vertebrates than to other invertebrate groups.

Atoms

Models of the Atom

The model of the atom has gone through several changes.

- In 1911, Ernest Rutherford proposed his nuclear theory of the atom, suggesting that an atom contains electrons and protons. At the time, no one understood how their opposite charges could exist together.
- In 1915, Niels Bohr proposed that electrons orbit the nucleus in the same way that planets orbit the sun. His model gained acceptance for a while, but it didn't explain some properties of some elements.
- In the 1920s, Erwin Schrödinger developed the current electron "cloud" model, which models the probability of finding an electron in a region outside the nucleus.

Cells

Cells into Tissues

Most multicellular organisms are made up of many different kinds of cells, each kind specialized to do a certain job. Cell specialization occurs during the development of a new organism. After fertilization, the genetic material contained in the zygote's nucleus directs each new cell produced by mitosis to enter one of several different pathways for development. In flowering plants, for example, a fertilized egg gives rise to at least 15 different kinds of specialized cells. In vertebrates, the egg gives rise to more than 100 specialized cell types. In both plants and animals, similar specialized cells that work together to carry out a specific task for the organism are known as a tissue.

Stages of Cell Division

Mitosis occurs in a predictable series of phases.

- **Interphase:** The cell prepares for cell division. The chromosomes copy themselves, and the cytoplasm of the cell increases in volume.
- **Prophase:** The chromosomes become thicker and visible with a microscope. The membrane surrounding the nucleus disappears.
- **Metaphase:** The chromosomes line up across the center of the cell.
- **Anaphase:** The chromosomes divide and move to opposite poles of the cell.
- **Telophase:** The end of mitosis. New nuclear membranes form around the chromosomes at each end of the cell. In animal cells, the cell membrane pinches in, dividing the cell into two identical daughter cells.

Changes in Matter

Changes in Matter

Cutting, bending, and wetting things with water are ways to cause physical changes in matter. When a physical change takes place, the substance itself does not change. Paper remains paper, no matter how it is changed physically. Matter can also be changed chemically, but chemical changes affect the basic nature of a substance. Chemical changes can occur when a substance burns, oxidizes, or is dissolved in an acid. When a chemical change takes place, a new substance is formed, and the change is permanent.

Gases

Like solids and liquids, gases are a form of matter with properties that can be observed and described. Gases spread out to fill whatever empty space they occupy, from balloons and bubbles to rooms, or Earth's atmosphere. Water vapor, oxygen, and carbon dioxide are some gases that students are familiar with. They can see carbon dioxide bubbles in soda water and oxygen bubbles on the ***elodea*** plant in fish tanks. They can observe water evaporate and become invisible as water vapor. Many gases are odorless and colorless, but others can smell like rotten eggs or swampy muck.

Students can experience how gases act when they squeeze an inflated balloon, open a bottle of soda water, or stand in front of a fan.

Climate

Climate

Recording and charting daily weather helps people understand the climate of an area. People make generalizations about climate based on recorded average weather conditions of an area over a long period of time. There are different kinds of climates, the three main types being polar, temperate, and tropical. In general, the greater a region's distance from the equator, the cooler the climate will be.

Earthquakes

Moment Magnitude Scale

The moment magnitude scale measures earthquake magnitude more precisely than the Richter Scale. The moment magnitude scale measures the total energy that an earthquake releases. This is measured by multiplying the distance the ground moves along the fault by the area of the fault's rupture surface. This scale is particularly accurate for measuring large earthquakes.

Seismology

The study of earthquake waves, known as ***seismology***, dates back almost 2,000 years to the Chinese. Today's seismographs work by suspending a weight from a support that is attached to bedrock.

- When waves from an earthquake reach the seismograph, the inertia of the weight keeps it stationary while Earth and the support vibrate.
- The vibrations used to be recorded on a rotating drum; now all seismographs are recorded digitally.
- The resulting record, called a seismogram, reveals two main types of waves: surface waves, which travel along Earth's surface, and the body waves, which travel through Earth's interior.

Earthquake Waves

An earthquake produces primary waves (P waves), secondary waves (S waves), and surface waves.

- P waves and S waves both travel through Earth's interior.
- P waves are "push-pull," or compression waves. They push (compress) and pull (expand) rocks in the same direction that the wave is moving. P waves can travel through solids, liquids, and gases.
- S waves, on the other hand, vibrate the particles at right angles to the waves' direction of travel. The vibrations can travel only through solids, so gases and liquids do not transmit S waves.
- Surface waves travel along Earth's outer layer, moving up and down and side to side. It is the side-to-side motion that is particularly damaging.

Earth's Changing Surface

Creep

Creep is a slow type of ground movement. During creep, soil gradually shifts downhill because of gravity. Unlike other types of ground movements such as landslides, creep is so slow that changes in landforms are hard to observe directly. The land may move only a few centimeters each year. But while creep cannot be seen occurring, over time it can move fences, utility poles, roads, and railroad tracks.

Types of Glaciers

There are two main kinds of glaciers. Valley glaciers are found in high mountain valleys. They flow slowly down mountainsides, eroding the mountain under them and forming U-shaped valleys. Only a few valley glaciers remain in North America, and even those are melting rapidly. Continental glaciers are ice sheets that cover large areas of Earth. They cover almost all of Greenland and Antarctica today. Thousands of years ago, when the global climate was colder, continental glaciers covered Europe, Canada, and the northern United States. The Great Lakes formed as retreating continental glaciers melted.

Erosion

Gravity is a force that pulls objects toward each other. It causes objects to fall toward Earth's surface and to roll down hills. Gravity can help erode mountains and hills by causing loose debris such as boulders and rocks to tumble down the slopes. Other agents, such as water, ice, wind, plants, and animals, also weather and erode rock, sand, and soil. In turn, rock, sand, and soil can further erode other rock. For example, a rolling boulder can cause erosion by breaking up rocks, causing material to fall, and destroying plants. Of all of the agents of erosion, water is the most powerful. A large drop of water can splash sand grains 30 cm (1 ft) or more into the air.

Ecosystems

How Animals Help Plants

Animals help plants in two basic ways. First, they help plants grow better. Animals enrich the soil by leaving behind their wastes. They also enrich it by mixing humus, or dead organic matter, into the soil. This helps recycle nutrients plants need to grow. Small animals, such as earthworms and moles, also aerate the soil when they dig tunnels. Plant roots get air and water more easily in loose, aerated soil. Animals also help plants make new plants. Some plants need animals to scatter plant seeds and pollen, which is necessary for reproduction. Many plants cannot make seeds unless they receive pollen from another plant, and they depend on animals such as insects, birds, and even some mammals to bring them the pollen they need. They produce sweet nectar to attract the animals to the part of the flower where the pollen is located.

Ecosystems

Scientists define an ecosystem as any group of organisms interacting with each other and with their physical environment. Thus, an ecosystem can be as small as a drop of pond water or as large as the entire Earth. The Earth ecosystem is called the biosphere. Organisms within an ecosystem compete with each other for food, energy, and space. They also interact with the nonliving components of the ecosystem, for example, by taking minerals from the soil, consuming water and oxygen, and anchoring topsoil against erosion.

Limiting Factors

In an ecosystem, all populations tend to increase until they reach the carrying capacity of the ecosystem. The carrying capacity is the number of organisms that the environment can support. Factors that limit this growth include the amounts of available food, water, oxygen, and space. Other factors include the number of predators, competition within a population, and parasitism. For plants, limiting factors also include the amount of sunlight, the richness of the soil, the temperature range, the strength of the winds, and so on. A factor that limits one population, such as scarce water limiting the growth of grass, can be an indirect limiting factor for the population that eats the grass—and for the population that eats the grass-eaters.

Primary Succession

Volcanoes that erupt periodically, such as those on the Hawaiian Islands, offer scientists a chance to study the stages of succession in an ecosystem. After a new lava flow, organisms immediately begin to arrive from nearby ecosystems. In Hawai'i, the first ones are likely to be wolf spiders. They eat other insects that wander onto the cooled lava. Soon the wind and rains bring seeds and spores that slip into cracks and pockets in the lava. The pockets catch rainwater, allowing ferns and shrubs to sprout. In time, these plants form a layer of vegetation, catching bits of leaves, bark, and roots from other plants. Decomposers help turn this dead matter into nutrients for more plants. In Hawai'i, a forest can develop on a lava flow in only 150 years.

Electricity

Electric Components

Most circuits use a few basic electric parts, also called components. Here are a few:

- Resistors are components that limit the amount of electric current that can flow. Limiting electrical currents in a circuit with a resistor is like using a smaller garden hose to limit the amount of water running through a hose.
- Capacitors are components that collect static charge on a plate so the static charge can be used at a later time to make an electric current.
- Transformers are like small electromagnets. They use electric current to make a magnetic field and then use the magnetic field to make an electric current in another wire.
- Transistors use an electric current through one wire to control the electric current going through another wire.

Uses of Static Electricity

If you have ever unloaded clothing from a dryer, you have probably seen and felt the effects of static electricity. Static electricity might seem like a nuisance, but it does have some practical uses. African American inventor Granville T. Woods invented a telegraph system in 1887 that used static electricity. In this system, messages were sent through static electricity created by a train to telegraph wires running beside the track. The messages then traveled along the wires to other trains and depots. The ability to send messages this way helped improve train safety. Today, one use of static electricity is in photocopy machines. Static electricity charges are applied to the ink so the ink sticks to the paper.

Conductors, Insulators, and Resistance

Some materials, called conductors, allow electric charges to move through them easily. Most metals are good conductors of electricity. That's why wires and the working parts of electrical outlets are made of metal. Other materials, called insulators, do not easily permit the flow of electricity. Rubber, plastic, and glass are insulators. Wires and electric plugs are covered in insulators for safety. Resistance is the degree to which any material resists the flow of electricity. Resistance (abbreviated R), is measured in ohms (Ω). A wire's thickness and length affect its resistance. Comparing the resistance of various wires requires that they be the same thickness and length.

Conductors and Insulators

Whether a material is a good electrical insulator or conductor depends on how easily negative charges move through the material. Metals are good conductors because their outer electrons are loosely bound and move freely through the material. The outer electrons in nonmetals, such as glass, rubber, wood, and plastic, are tightly bound. The repulsion of electrons added to the materials is not enough to push the outer electrons through the material. A stream of water is attracted or repelled by a charged object because its molecules have a positive and negative end. However, pure water is an insulator. When salts dissolve in water, they form ions—charged particles that can move freely through the water. The ions will then conduct electricity.

Electromagnetism

Until the 1800s, electricity and magnetism were thought to be separate forces. Experimental evidence then began to accumulate, suggesting that electricity and magnetism are actually two aspects of the same phenomenon. In 1905, Einstein's theory of relativity confirmed the dual nature of a single electromagnetic force. We encounter this dual nature in visible light, ultraviolet radiation, microwaves, and radio waves. We use it in practical applications in which magnetic fields generate current electricity (generators) and current electricity produces magnetic fields (electromagnets).

Energy

Energy

The scientific definition of ***energy*** is "the ability to cause changes in matter." Without energy, matter does not change. Energy can be divided into two broad categories: kinetic energy and potential energy. Kinetic energy is the energy of motion. Anything that is moving has kinetic energy. Potential energy is stored energy. An object that has potential energy has the potential to move or change. A book on a shelf has potential energy—it could fall to the floor. A child on the raised end of a seesaw has potential energy—she could drop back to the ground. In these cases, the object gained potential energy as it was raised into its position. The higher an object is raised, the more potential energy it acquires.

Energy Resources

Energy resources are crucial factors in our economic and political systems as well as in our daily lives. For 150 years, most of humanity's energy has come from fossil fuels—oil, coal, and natural gas. Because these fuels take so long to form, supplies are finite. Remedies such as finding new reserves and reducing demand will work for a while, but they only delay the inevitable. At some point, people will have to switch to renewable energy resources such as wind power and solar power. Before this can happen, technological advances are required to make these renewable sources as powerful and efficient as current sources.

Forms of Energy

There are ways to categorize different forms of energy other than as potential and kinetic energy. Energy that comes from the sun is called solar energy. Solar energy itself consists of many different kinds of electromagnetic energy—infrared, light, ultraviolet, radio waves, gamma rays, and X rays. (All of these are electromagnetic waves; each has a different wavelength.) Other forms of energy include chemical energy, mechanical energy, electrical energy, and sound energy. In both technology and everyday life, energy is constantly changing from one form to another.

Heat Transfer

All matter in the universe is made of atoms and molecules. These particles have kinetic energy; they are always moving. The particles of a solid stay in a fixed place and vibrate. The particles of a liquid slide easily past each other. The particles of a gas fly all over the place. This form of random, kinetic energy is called thermal energy. The average amount of thermal energy in all the particles of a substance is the substance's temperature. The higher the temperature, the more thermal energy there is and the more movement there is. Natural movement of thermal energy is called heat, and it can occur in one of three ways—by conduction, convection, or radiation. If two substances contact each other, thermal energy will move from the warmer substance to the cooler one; this is conduction.

Mechanical Energy

The term ***mechanical energy*** is sometimes used to describe kinetic energy, or energy of motion. For example, falling water has mechanical energy. This mechanical energy can move a turbine. The turbine changes the mechanical energy to electric energy. Or, perhaps a person turns a crank on a generator. The mechanical energy of the turning crank is changed into electric energy. The mechanical energy of two sticks rubbing together is turned into heat energy by friction. The mechanical energy of a spring uncoiling makes a wind-up toy move. Although not technically correct, this meaning often appears in textbooks. You may need to explain this to students who are confused by the conflicting definitions.

Engineering and Technology

Engineering

Engineering is the use of science knowledge to design products that solve problems and meet people's needs and wants. The products of engineering are ***technology***. Technology can be as simple as a pencil or as complex as a car or computer. We're used to thinking of technology as only high-tech electronics. Actually, nearly everything that we see on a daily basis came from a factory that was designed by engineers—paper, aluminum cans, plastic cups, mirrors, roads, cars, fabric, ink pens, and on and on. Processes are also technology, for example, the steps for making steel, a cookie recipe, or a trouble-shooting script for computer hardware.

Engineering Design Process

The Engineering Design Process

Engineers often follow an iterative design process to develop a solution to a problem. The steps of the process vary and the divisions between steps are somewhat arbitrary. *ScienceFusion* uses a simplified five-step engineering design process:

1. **Find a Problem** Identify a problem; describe an unmet need or want and who will use the solution.
2. **Plan and Build** Decide the criteria the solution must meet to succeed; brainstorm designs; consider constraints, or limitations, such as budget, size, weight, and available materials; choose materials; draw detailed plans; and finally, construct a prototype.
3. **Test and Improve** Test the prototype against the design criteria. If it is successful, make improvements to enhance its performance.
4. **Redesign** Often, the first attempt at a solution fails to meet the design criteria. Engineers take what they learned from testing and start over with a new design.
5. **Communicate** Document work throughout the process and communicate with team members. At the end of the process, engineers share the final design, explain the test results, and often write directions for how to use the product.

Exploring Space

Mars

People dream about space travel to other planets. Many scientists are now considering the possibility of humans traveling to Mars.

- The distance from Earth to Mars is approximately 80,000,000 km (49,700,000 mi). The trip would take a spacecraft many months to complete.
- Two rovers, ***Spirit*** and ***Opportunity,*** arrived on Mars in January 2004. Each rover carries a sophisticated set of instruments that allows it to search for evidence that liquid water may have been present on Mars in the past.
- Mars has an atmosphere that would not support life as we know it. NASA hopes to change that with ambitious plans to thicken the atmosphere of Mars and even melt its polar ice caps.

Trip to the Moon

- The *Saturn V* rocket had three stages. Each stage was mounted on top of the previous stage. The first stage produced more than 33 million N of thrust at liftoff.
- A command and service module (CSM) at the top of the *Saturn V* carried three astronauts into space and toward the moon. The CSM traveled the 384,000 km (about 239,000 mi) from Earth to the moon in four days.
- For comparison, it takes about four days to drive a car across the continental United States, a distance of about 5,000 kilometers (about 3,100 miles).

Food Chains and Food Webs

Food Chains and Food Webs

Organisms get the energy they need from food. A food chain traces the path of energy as it moves from one organism to the next in an ecosystem. In most ecosystems, energy begins with the sun, so producers (organisms that use the sun's energy to make food) always form the base, or starting point, of a food chain. Arrows are typically used to show the direction of energy movement in a food chain.

A food chain only shows one energy path in an ecosystem. But most organisms are part of more than one food chain. Scientists often use a food web to show a more complete picture of the flow of energy in an ecosystem. A food web is a system of several overlapping food chains.

In most ecosystems, the energy starts with the sun. This energy is taken in by producers (plants) and converted to food energy. The energy in food moves through different levels of consumers. The first to feed on plants is a primary consumer. The secondary consumers feed on primary consumers. A third feeder is the tertiary consumer. The final link is filled by bacteria and fungi that act as decomposers. These organisms feed on and break down the remains of consumers when they die.

Forces

Force

Force is what makes all objects move. Force can be either a push or a pull. Force can start or stop motion, speed up or slow down motion, or change the direction of motion. When a child slides down a slide, gravity pulls him toward Earth. When a child pushes a toy truck, her muscles contract and pull her bones to make her arm move and push. When a flag is blowing and waving, the wind is pushing it back and forth.

Units of Force

Standardized units of measurement, such as centimeters for length, have been developed to make measurements consistent everywhere. There are two common systems—the customary (English) system, and the SI (metric) system. Scientists generally use the SI, or metric, system. SI units of mass are grams and kilograms. Because weight is a measure of force between objects, units of weight are also units of force. In the English system, the unit of force is pounds. In the SI system, it is newtons, abbreviated N and named for Isaac Newton. A newton is defined as the force needed to accelerate a 1-kg mass 1 m/s^2.

Fossils

Fossil Formation

Fossils rarely form. Whether plant or animal remains become fossils depends on what the organism is, where it lived, and whether the remains were protected from exposure. Organisms that are buried quickly and remain protected from air, water, bacteria, and scavengers are more likely to become fossils, because the remains will not be eaten and they will not decay too quickly. Hard materials such as bones, teeth, wood, and shells are more likely to become fossils than soft tissues. Marine organisms are more likely to become fossils than land-dwelling organisms. In a few cases, organisms such as woolly mammoths (prehistoric elephant-like animals) were preserved intact when they froze in the Arctic tundra.

Dinosaur Trace Fossils

When most people think of dinosaur fossils, they think of bones and large skeletons. Such "body fossils" are not the only types of fossil evidence, however. A trace fossil is indirect evidence of ancient life. It is not a body part but evidence of an organism's behavior. Examples of trace fossils left by dinosaurs include tracks, tooth marks, eggs, nests, gastroliths, and coprolites. A coprolite is fossilized animal droppings. Dinosaur coprolites reveal what dinosaurs consumed. Coprolites can contain either body fossils of plant material (indicating a herbivorous diet) or bones (indicating a carnivorous diet). Gastroliths, or "gizzard stones," can be difficult to distinguish from polished stones. Those most easily identified are found in the rib cages of dinosaur skeletons, which is where the dinosaur's stomach was.

Paleontology

Paleontology is the study of ancient life through analysis of plant and animal fossils.

- Paleontologists focus on the biology of ancient life. Their work involves investigating ancient life, trying to discover its connection to current life forms on Earth, and developing an understanding of the ancient forms' interrelationship with their environment.
- Paleontologists are also concerned with geology and have a major influence in determining the facts about the layers of rock that make up Earth. Using index fossils and other information about the rocks in which fossils occur, paleontologists aid petroleum geologists in their search for oil and gas.

Heredity

Nature Versus Nurture

- Behavior is the response of an organism to its surroundings.
- Behavior may be inherited—passed from parent to offspring—or learned.
- Instincts are behaviors that are inherited responses to stimuli and do not require learning. In newborn humans, instincts include crying.
- Some instinctive behaviors are influenced by learning. For example, a tiger is born with the instinct to hunt, but it must learn skills to hunt effectively.
- Learned behaviors are acquired completely as a result of experience. In humans, reading is a learned behavior.

Human Body

Parts of the Skeleton

The human skeleton is divided into two parts: the axial skeleton and the appendicular skeleton. The axial skeleton contains the bones that make up the face, skull, rib cage, and vertebral column. The main function of the axial skeleton is to protect vital organs of the body, such as the brain, heart, and spinal cord. The remaining bones of the skeleton make up the appendicular skeleton.

Bones

About 206 bones together form the human skeleton. The head bones make up the skull, which sits on top of the spine. At the top of the spine sit the shoulder bones, which are linked to the arm bones. Twelve pairs of rib bones curve around the spine and connect at the front of the chest. At the bottom of the spine, pelvic bones connect to the leg bones. At birth, a human baby has as many as 350 bones in its body, yet an adult has only 206 bones. The difference is due to the fusing of certain bones that occurs as humans mature. The places where bones meet are called **joints**. Knuckle and knee joints act like hinges and can bend naturally in only one way. Ball-and-socket joints in the shoulders and hips allow bones to move in a complete circle. There are more than 600 **muscles** in the human body. Some of these work under voluntary control, such as arm and thigh muscles. Others, such as those in the stomach, are involuntary.

How Bodies Grow

The human body grows, changing in both shape and size, from infancy to about the age of 20. Growth is rapid during the first year of life. Weight will triple and height will increase by one half before a child turns one. When a baby is born, its head is 25% of its total body height. As the baby grows, the body's proportions will change. Arms, legs and torso grow so that the head becomes 12.5% of the body's size in an adult. During childhood, the growth rate is steady. It speeds up again between the ages of 10 and 16 when the child's body matures and becomes adult. This stage is called puberty. The adult body does not change much but may experience weight gain, shrinking, skin wrinkles, and loss of hair and muscle.

The Five Senses

The five senses are sight, hearing, smell, touch, and taste. Receptors for each sense are found on our faces in our eyes, ears, noses, mouths, and skin. Receptors for the sense of touch are also found in the skin on all parts of our bodies. Our senses send signals about their environment to the brain through the nervous system. The brain then processes the information from the senses. This enables us to learn about the world and to make decisions. The senses are survival tools because they send signals to the brain that help us detect danger and pain.

Human Organ Systems

In addition to its solo function, each organ in the human body is also a part of an ***organ system***. The human body has 11 organ systems; each carries out specific tasks for the body. The function of six systems is as follows: the circulatory system carries oxygen and nutrients to cells of the body; the respiratory system exchanges carbon dioxide for oxygen; the skeletal system provides support, protects internal organs, and produces blood cells; the muscular system allows the body to move and produces heat to keep it warm; the nervous system directs activities of all systems and responds to stimuli; the excretory system eliminates wastes from the body.

Inquiry Skills

Inferring and Concluding

The word *infer* is often defined as "concluding by reason." Students may have difficulty distinguishing between inferring and concluding.

- In scientific inquiry, drawing a conclusion is deciding whether an experiment supports the hypothesis being tested.
- *Inferring* is used in a much less specific way to describe reasoning from specific evidence to a general conclusion. For example, if one observes a bus arrive at the same corner at almost the same time each morning, one can infer that the bus is on a regular route and is following a schedule. No experiment is necessary, unless one wishes to convert the inference to a hypothesis and test it.

The Null Hypothesis

It may not occur to students that a hypothesis does not have to imply a difference. A null hypothesis can be used.

- A hypothesis might state that a round parachute, rather than parachutes of other shapes, will be better at keeping an egg from breaking. A null hypothesis might be that the shape of the parachute will make no difference.
- Often, scientists will state a null hypothesis because it helps prevent them from looking for a certain outcome. For example, they might test round parachutes and square ones, without stating that either type will be better.

What Is a Model?

Students may think that a model is always a small version of something larger. Point out that a model does not have to be a real object that they build.

- A model can be an idea that they get from nature, such as the way a leaf falls. When people first tried to fly, they thought of birds as models. They tried to make airplanes look and behave like birds.
- Sometimes people get ideas for models from things that are very different from the problem they're trying to solve. The man who invented Velcro got his idea from burrs that stuck to his clothes when he walked through some weeds!

Landforms

What Are Landforms?

Landforms are natural features that make up Earth's surface. There are many kinds of landforms, including mountains, hills, valleys, plains, plateaus, beaches, and dunes. Some landforms, such as mountains and plateaus, form as a result of upward movement of rock. Mountains can be found both on the ocean floor and on land. Other landforms are caused by erosion and by deposition of earth materials. Canyons are narrow, deep gorges that are cut into Earth by the action of running water, while valleys can be the result of erosion by streams and rivers and by glacial action. Landforms can also be caused by the movement of Earth's crust and by volcanic activity.

Light

Properties of Light

When light strikes a surface, the light may be reflected, refracted, or absorbed. What happens to light depends on the surface it hits. When light hits a smooth, shiny surface, it is reflected, or thrown back. Reflected light enables you to see yourself in a mirror. When light passes from one substance into another, it is refracted, or bent. That is why an object partially immersed in water appears to bend at the water line. Many surfaces absorb light. Some surfaces are opaque. They don't let light pass through, and you can't see through them. Surfaces that let some light through, such as wax paper, are translucent. Surfaces that let most light through are transparent. You can see through them.

Lasers

Laser light is very different from regular light.

- Laser light is **monochromatic**. It contains one specific wavelength of light. The color depends on the type of material used to make the laser.
- Laser light released is **coherent**—the light waves move as one, similar to the feet of marching soldiers, rather than moving off randomly.
- The light is **directional**. A laser has a very narrow beam that is bright and tight. Light from a flashlight, by contrast, spreads out.

Although laser light spreads out a little as it travels from the source, it has been used to measure the distance to the moon. Astronauts left a mirror on the moon. Scientists aim a laser at the reflector to measure how long the light takes to reach the moon and return.

Visible Light

Visible light is the small range of electromagnetic waves to which the human eye is sensitive. Visible light ranges from red, with a wavelength of about 7×10^{-5} cm, to violet, with a wavelength of about 4×10^{-5} cm. When all the wavelengths are present, the effect is white light.

- All electromagnetic waves, including visible light, travel at about 300 million meters per second through a vacuum.
- When electrons are energized, they move to higher energy levels farther from the nucleus. As they return to lower energy levels, they emit energy of various wavelengths, some of which can be visible light. In the visible light spectrum, red has the longest wavelength and lowest frequency. Violet has the shortest wavelength and highest frequency.

Waves

Waves are part of our daily experience, although we cannot always see them. The sounds we hear and the light we see are waves. Waves are regular, repeating disturbances or deformations. For example, we hear sounds because of pressure deformations of the air, water, or other medium. The waves "propagate" through the medium. Electromagnetic waves such as visible light and radio waves can travel through space. There are several different types of waves. Longitudinal waves vibrate in the same direction as they are traveling. Sound waves are an example of longitudinal waves. Electromagnetic waves are transverse. They vibrate at right angles to the direction of travel. We can also classify waves as traveling or standing. Traveling waves move, while standing waves oscillate in place and do not travel.

Magnetism

Magnets

A magnet is a solid, such as a piece of metal or a stone, that attracts objects that are made of iron or of steel, which contains iron. Natural magnets, called ***magnetite*** or ***lodestone***, are formed inside Earth. Centuries ago, sailors navigated by suspending a lodestone from a string to detect North. Today, magnets are found in computers and many appliances. They activate speakers in televisions, radios, stereos, and telephones. They are used as door latches and to separate items in recycling centers. To avoid damage, do not place magnets near computers or software. Do not drop, strike, or heat magnets, as demagnetization can result. Magnets attract only iron and a few other metals, such as nickel and cobalt.

Magnetic Force

Magnets can be used to make some things move, even without touching them, because magnetic force reaches beyond the magnet. This area where the force extends is called the magnetic field. How far the force reaches, or the size of the magnetic field, depends on a magnet's strength. Most magnets used by students have small fields extending an inch or less. Earth has a magnetic field that extends more than 37,000 miles into space. Magnetic force happens in an iron object when groups of atoms, called domains, align. The domains cause an electromagnetic force that reaches beyond the object. The force is strongest within the magnet, and decreases as distance from the magnet increases. Scientists hypothesize that Earth's magnetic force comes from its core of hot iron surrounded by a fluid outer core.

Magnetic Poles

The poles of a magnet are named for the direction in which they point. Thus, a bar magnet suspended from a string tied around its center will swing until its north-seeking pole points north and the south-seeking pole points south. If a bar magnet is broken into two pieces, each piece will have its own north- and south-seeking poles. The poles of disk and circular magnets are not as easy to identify. For example, ring magnets can be magnetized so the inner edge is one pole, and the outer edge, the other pole; the two surfaces of a disk magnet may be the poles, and so on.

Measuring Matter

Mass and Weight

The mass and weight of an object are not the same; they are different properties. Mass is the amount of matter an object has. Weight is the amount of pull that gravity has on an object. The mass of an object stays the same regardless of where it is. Its weight can change depending on the strength of the gravitational force that is pulling on it. An object would weigh more on Earth than on the moon because Earth has more gravity than the moon. Mass is measured with a balance. Weight is measured with a scale.

Meteorology

Anemometers and Hygrometers

An anemometer is a tool that measures wind speed. One kind of anemometer has four cups connected at right angles to an upright shaft. The wind pushes the cups, which causes the shaft to turn. A system of gears converts the number of turns per minute into wind speed. Another kind of anemometer has an L-shaped tube, with one end open to the flow of air and the other end connected to a device that measures the pressure of the air blowing into it. Hygrometers measure humidity. A hair hygrometer, for example, measures the changes in length of a human hair that occur due to the absorption of water. The hair gets longer in humid air and shorter in dry air.

Clouds and Rain

Liquid water is constantly evaporating from Earth's surface. When water evaporates, it changes to a gas called ***water vapor***. Water vapor condenses back to a liquid in the form of tiny droplets after 9 or 10 days. These tiny droplets make up clouds, or fog, or the dew we see on grass in the morning. If the tiny droplets form a cloud, and conditions allow, then the droplets grow until they are heavy enough to fall back to Earth as precipitation. Depending on the temperature conditions, precipitation can fall as either rain, snow, or ice, which might be either sleet or hail. About three-fourths of all Earth's precipitation falls over the ocean. The rest soaks into the ground or runs off into streams and rivers that flow into the ocean. Before long, the sun's heat causes the water to evaporate again, and the water cycle repeats.

Wind

Moving air is called wind. The whole body of air surrounding Earth is constantly moving, in part because of Earth's spin, and because of an uneven distribution of heat in Earth's land and water. Since air is a gas, it expands and contracts according to its temperature and the temperature of whatever it moves across. Air over warm regions that has been heated by strong sunshine is less dense than air over cooler regions. The greater the difference in density between the two air masses, the faster the wind will move. This movement, plus the more complicated movements caused by Earth's spin, produces wind conditions that affect our weather. Wind can be both harmful and helpful. Strong unpredictable winds such as those found in hurricanes or tornadoes can be life threatening, if people do not take shelter. But predictable, steady winds can be helpful when people use them to power wind turbines that generate electricity.

Fronts

Cold fronts and warm fronts are only two types of fronts. Sometimes the cold and warm air masses remain in the same position, or are stationary, for a time. The boundary dividing these air masses is a ***stationary front***. Locations along a stationary front may have the same weather for days. Differences in air temperature occur in locations on either side of the front. Sometimes a warm air mass is trapped between two cold air masses to form an ***occluded front***. This occurs because cold fronts travel about twice as fast as warm fronts travel.

Earth's Magnetosphere

Earth is surrounded by a large magnetic field that protects it from harmful, charged-particle radiation from the sun. It is a magnetosphere.

- The magnetic north and south poles of Earth's magnetosphere are close to—not directly over—the North Pole and the South Pole of Earth.
- When charged particles from the sun run into the magnetosphere, the magnetic field catches the particles, causing them to be funneled toward the magnetic north and south poles.
- The southern lights—*aurora australis*—form around Earth's South Pole. They are seen less frequently than the northern lights because fewer people live at the magnetic south pole.

Minerals

Minerals

There are more than 2,000 known minerals on Earth. For a material to be classified as a mineral, it must meet certain requirements. The material must be a solid, naturally occurring substance that has a definite chemical composition and internal arrangement of atoms, which is reflected in the mineral's outward appearance when the mineral has enough space to grow. The chemical makeup is responsible for the mineral's color, crystal shape, hardness, luster, streak, and other properties. People often think of minerals as gems, but not all minerals are gems. Many minerals are metal ores and salts. Likewise, not all gems are minerals. For example, pearls and amber are both produced through biological processes.

Motion

Action-Reaction Forces

Students may wonder how forces produce acceleration if there is always an equal but opposite reaction force. Point out the following facts:

- Forces are balanced only if they act on the ***same*** object.
- Action-reaction forces act on ***different*** objects.

If you push a box across the floor, the box pushes back on you with an equal but opposite force. However, your mass is greater than that of the box, so there is a net force on the box that makes it move.

Laws of Motion

Sir Isaac Newton was an English physicist and mathematician who lived from 1643 to 1727. He formulated three fundamental laws of motion. These laws state that (1) an object at rest will remain at rest, and an object in motion will continue to move at the same speed and direction unless acted upon by an external force; (2) an external force acting on an object causes acceleration, and the amount of acceleration depends on the strength of the force and the mass of the object; and (3) for every force there is an equal and opposite force. In the twentieth century, quantum physics and Albert Einstein's theory of relativity suggested that Newton's laws of motion do not apply to atomic and subatomic particles or to objects moving close to the speed of light.

Relative Motion

Everything in the universe, from atoms to galaxies, is moving. Even objects on the surface of Earth that appear to be standing still, such as buildings, are moving from west to east at about 1600 km/hr (1000 mi/hr) as Earth rotates. Therefore, the motion of an object must be measured relative to other objects. For example:

- A passenger seated in a bus may not be moving with respect to the bus but moving with respect to the road on which the bus is traveling. The person is moving at yet another speed with respect to Earth.
- People riding in trains going in opposite directions find it difficult to judge whether their train, the other train, or both are moving, because they have no stationary frame of reference.

Natural Resources

Energy Resources

Natural resources that provide people with energy are called *energy resources.* Sunlight is an energy resource that provides light and heat. The energy of sunlight can also be changed into electricity. Other energy resources include wind (moving air), tidal or current (moving water), and fuels such as wood, coal, gasoline, and oil.

Material Resources

Minerals, water, plants, animals, rocks, and soil are all *material resources*. Some of these things can be used to make different products. For example, sand is used to make glass, and wheat kernels are ground up to make flour. Renewable resources are those that are regularly replaced or replenished by nature. Plants, animals, and water are **renewable resources**. Plants and animals reproduce to make more of their own kind. Thus when some plants are harvested, new plants can be grown to take their place. Water is replaced through the water cycle. Some natural resources are forever lost when used. Others take many years to be replaced by natural processes. **Nonrenewable resources** are those that can be used only once, or those that are not replaced by nature nearly as quickly as they are used. Oil, coal, and natural gas are considered nonrenewable resources because it takes millions of years for them to form. Minerals, including metals, are also considered nonrenewable resources. All natural resources must be used with care. Nonrenewable resources can be used up, making them unavailable to people in the future. Even renewable resources can be polluted or destroyed if not treated carefully.

Oceans

Ocean Plants and Animals

Algae are plantlike organisms that live in the oceans. They are not considered to be true plants because they have no transport system to carry water and nutrients. Algae include seaweeds and kelp. Some, such as kelp, can grow up to 30.5 m (100 ft) long. Others are single cells and can be seen only with a microscope. Ocean animals live where they can meet their needs. Most ocean plants and animals live in or near shallow water or near the surface of the open ocean.

Oceans and Sea Water

One large body of water covers almost three-fourths of Earth's surface. This body of water is separated into five regions—the Pacific, Atlantic, Indian, Southern, and Arctic Oceans. The largest ocean is the Pacific Ocean. It covers a third of Earth's surface and extends from the Arctic Ocean to Antarctica's Ross Sea. It contains about half of all the water on Earth. Oceans border all of Earth's large landmasses.

Salinity

The Arctic and Southern Oceans are less salty than other saltwater seas and oceans for several reasons, including freshwater precipitation, low evaporation, and melting of the ice. By checking the salinity of the water and the expected temperatures, scientists can predict when ice will form around ships and in harbors. Ocean water contains, in some amount, all the elements found on Earth. The seven most abundant elements in seawater are chlorine, sodium, magnesium, sulfur, calcium, potassium, and bromine. They make up 99 percent of ocean salinity, with the other elements present in trace amounts. Scientists estimate that these trace amounts include about 9 million tons of gold!

Planetary Cycles

Rotation and Revolution

Earth has two primary motions within the solar system. It rotates, or spins, on its axis once every 23 hours, 56 minutes, 4.1 seconds. A point at the equator spins at about 1,600 km per hour (about 1,000 mph); a point at 45° North rotates more slowly at approximately 1,073 km per hour (about 667 mph). In addition to its spinning motion, Earth is also revolving around the sun in an elliptical orbit. Traveling through space at about 106,000 km per hour (66,000 mph), it takes approximately 365 days for Earth to make one complete revolution around the sun, the length of one year. Every four years, the calendar includes an extra day to accommodate the additional time.

Plants

Flowers

The blossoms of flowers are often arranged in groups. They appear in tightly packed clusters, broad clusters, or along a single stalk, such as the puya. The ***puya*** is an ancient treelike angiosperm that grows in the Andes Mountains of South America. Its flowers form spikes of up to 8000 bright-green blossoms. This plant, classified as a bromeliad, forms flowerstalks that can be nearly 5.4 m (18 ft) tall.

Roots

The two basic root systems found in plants are a taproot system and a fibrous root system. In a taproot system, such as in a carrot, a large root grows down into the soil, producing smaller lateral roots. A fibrous root system, such as in grasses, begins with a primary root that is shortly replaced by many roots that form from the stem. Both root systems have adaptations to perform certain functions. For example, taproots of beets and carrots are modified to store food. In mangrove trees, large, woody prop roots develop from adventitious roots on horizontal branches.

Tropism

The response of a plant to stimuli in its environment is called *tropism*. This response is triggered by plant hormones called *auxins*. A plant that grows toward a stimulus is said to display a positive tropism, while one that grows away from a stimulus displays a negative tropism. Most plants show tropisms to light, or phototropism, and gravity, or gravitropism. The root displays a positive gravitropism and a negative phototropism. As the stem grows upward, it shows a negative gravitropism and a positive phototropism.

Unusual Pollinators

The tiny Australian honey possum feeds on pollen and nectar from desert flowers such as the ***Banksia*** and, in the process, pollinates the plants. The South American creeper is a plant that gives off a bad odor that attracts flies. When a fly enters the flower, it becomes trapped overnight. During its "incarceration," the fly pollinates the plant. The flower fades by morning and the fly escapes.

Photosynthesis

Photosynthesis is a series of chemical reactions that plants and some protists and bacteria use to convert solar energy into chemical energy. The basic photosynthetic reaction converts six molecules of water and six molecules of carbon dioxide into one molecule of glucose (sugar) and six molecules of oxygen. Chlorophyll and other pigments enable the chemical reaction by absorbing energy from different wavelengths of sunlight. Additional chemical reactions convert and store the glucose as complex sugars and starches.

Plant Adaptation

An adaptation is a characteristic of a plant or an animal that allows the organism to survive in a particular environment. Some adaptations have developed over many generations. Some, however, occur within a single generation. The key to adaptation is variation, or difference, within a species. In order for a species to survive, it must be able to adapt, or change, to better fit new circumstances that arise within an environment.

Types of Plants

Plants can be divided into two groups—flowering plants and nonflowering plants. Flowering plants have special parts that make seeds. Seeds are the first stage of growth for many plants. Roses and lilies are kinds of plants that have flowers. A conifer is one type of nonflowering plant. Conifers are plants that have cones instead of flowers. The seeds are made inside of cones which hold and protect the seeds. After some time, the seeds will be ready to grow into new plants. When this happens, the cone will open and the seeds will fall out. Most conifers have needle-shaped leaves that stay green all year. Many conifers do not shed their leaves like other plants. Pines, spruce, firs, cypress, and yews are kinds of conifers.

What Plants Need

Plants need light, water, and air to produce food through a process called ***photosynthesis***. This process takes place in a plant's leaves and green stems. These parts contain chlorophyll, which enables the plant to use water, carbon dioxide from the air, and light energy from the sun to make sugars. Plants then use the sugar to grow and to form flowers, seeds, and fruit, which enables them to reproduce. Soil supplies nutrients, which are certain chemical elements that plants need to live. Plants grown hydroponically, or in a growing solution, get these nutrients from the solution. Plants that grow aeroponically, or in air, get the nutrients and moisture they need from air.

Plant Nutrients

All plants need certain chemical elements to live. Elements they need in large amounts, called macronutrients, include carbon, hydrogen, oxygen, sulfur, phosphorus, nitrogen, potassium, calcium, and magnesium. Nutrients needed in smaller amounts, called micronutrients, include copper, zinc, iron, nickel, and other minerals. Plants get oxygen and carbon through their leaves and absorb other elements through their roots. Most root absorption takes place from the soil; however, plants grown hydroponically, or in water, obtain the minerals they need from a mineral-rich growing solution. Plants grown aeroponically, or in air, have their roots sprayed with a mineral-rich solution.

Plant Parts

Plants have parts that are adapted to get what the plant needs. Most roots grow underground and absorb water and nutrients. Roots also anchor the plant. Some roots, called taproots, are thick. Other roots, called fibrous roots, are thin and spread out. Stems support a plant's leaves and flowers and improve the plant's ability to absorb water and nutrients. Some stems, such as tree trunks and limbs, are woody. Leaves make most of the food that the plant needs in a process called photosynthesis. The leaves contain chlorophyll, which enables them to use light energy to combine water and carbon dioxide to make the plant's food. Some plants reproduce from seeds. Seed plants are divided into two main groups. In flowering plants, the fruit protects the seeds. In conifers, such as pines and firs, seeds are made in cones.

Seeds

Seeds contain the food they need to start the growing process, but they have three other requirements for continued growth—warmth, oxygen, and water. The roots are necessary for further plant development. Seeds use their stored food to initiate sprouting. They absorb water through their covers from the soil. They get oxygen from air, which is trapped between soil particles. Warmth is usually provided by the sun.

Parts of a Seed

Seeds come in many different sizes, shapes, and colors. The outside of a seed is the seed coat. This covering protects the seed. Some seeds, such as those of the coconut palm, have additional protection in the form of shells or husks. The fleshy part of the seed, called the cotyledon, is food for the embryo, which is the beginning of a new plant. The radicle is the first part of the plant to grow from the seed. It is the root of the plant embryo. The radicle holds the seedling in the soil and absorbs water that the seedling needs for growth. The shoot, which consists of both stems and leaves, emerges after the root.

Fruit

Most fruits contain seeds. Through fruits, plants are able to disperse their seeds with the help of various animals. Oranges, cherries, and tomatoes are all considered a type of berry. Blackberries and strawberries are a different type of berry. Both types ripen into a sweet, moist fruit, which is attractive to the animals that eat them. Then the seeds pass, unharmed, through the animal's digestive tract and are deposited on the soil in a new location. Fruits are an important part of the human diet because they provide the body with vitamins, such as vitamin C, and dietary fiber. Humans eat fruit in the forms of fresh fruit, jams, jellies, and pickles. Fruits can be packed in cans or jars or frozen to preserve them or transport them.

Plate Tectonics

Plate Tectonics

According to the theory of plate tectonics, Earth's outer shell consists of about 20 rigid plates (seven of these are major plates). The plates are moving continuously, although very slowly, at a rate of only a few centimeters a year. Most of the large plates include both continental and oceanic crust. In general, continental crust is thick and oceanic crust is thin. Each plate moves as a distinct unit, so interactions between plates occur along plate boundaries. There are divergent boundaries, convergent boundaries, and transform fault boundaries. A plate is often bounded by a combination of these zones.

Plate Boundaries

At the spreading center of a divergent boundary, plates are moving apart. New crust is constantly being produced by magma pushing up from the mantle. However, because the total surface area of Earth remains constant, crust must also be reabsorbed into the mantle. This can happen where two plates collide along a convergent boundary, or the edges of the plates can fold and bend forming mountain ranges. One plate is subducted, that is, it sinks below the other. At a transform fault boundary, plates grind past one another without producing or subducting crust. Movement along these faults often causes earthquakes. The San Andreas fault zone in California is an example.

Properties of Matter

Chemical Properties and Changes

The chemical properties of a substance include what it is composed of and what chemical changes it can undergo.

- A chemical change is independent of physical properties. For example, hydrogen and helium are both colorless gases at room temperature. However, hydrogen reacts with many other elements and compounds.
- In a chemical change, one or more substances are converted into one or more new substances. When pennies tarnish, some of the copper and zinc atoms in them combine with oxygen, forming metal oxides. The compounds are chemically different from either of the elements that formed them and also have different properties.

Density

The density of a material is a measure of how close together its matter is packed. An object with a low density, such as a block of balsa wood, floats because its material is less dense than water. The opposite is true of a high density object, such as a golf ball. A golf ball sinks because it is denser than water. A large ship can float because its mass is spread out and a large part of its volume is air, so its average density is lower than that of water.

Matter

Matter refers to everything in the universe that occupies space and has mass. Matter is made up of microscopic particles called atoms. Matter generally exists in three states: solid, liquid, and gas. Although there is a fourth state called plasma, it is not common in our everyday world. Each kind of matter can be identified by its specific properties, or special qualities, such as smell, taste, size, shape, color, mass, and solubility. All matter shares two properties: taking up space and having mass. However, two objects cannot occupy the same place at the same time. All substances are made from more than 110 different elements, which, when combined differently, produce millions of materials with different properties.

Rocks

Rocks and How They Are Used

Rocks are naturally occurring solid objects made of one or more minerals. Rocks are found all over the surface of Earth, from the tops of mountains to the ocean floor. They vary in color, depending on the kinds of minerals in them, or in texture, depending on the size of the mineral grains. Earth's crust is made up of three different groups of rocks. Igneous rocks form when molten rock such as magma or lava cools. Granite and basalt are types of igneous rocks. Sedimentary rocks form when sediments are cemented together or when chemicals precipitate from ocean water. Sandstone, limestone, and shale are types of sedimentary rock. Metamorphic rocks form when any type of rock is subjected to enough heat and pressure to change it without melting. Slate and marble are types of metamorphic rock. Most kinds of rocks can easily be found in one region of the world or another. People use rocks for building roads and structures, as well as for jewelry and other products, including materials such as chalk.

Rocks and the Rock Cycle

Igneous rocks are formed when molten rock cools and solidifies beneath the surface. On Earth's surface, any type of rock can weather and the sediment be deposited in layers, often in the ocean. Over a long time, the sediment fuses and becomes sedimentary rock. If pulled deep inside Earth, any type of rock can be converted to metamorphic rock through great heat and pressure (but not great enough to melt rock).

Weathering

Weathering is the process that changes the surface of rocks. There are two types of weathering, physical and chemical. During physical weathering, rocks are broken down into smaller rocks by force. One example of physical weathering is when water seeps into the cracks of large rocks. When this water freezes, it expands and breaks the rock into smaller pieces. Plant roots can also grow in the cracks of rocks and cause weathering. Physical weathering can also be caused by thermal expansion, which is the constant heating and cooling of rocks. Chemical weathering is when the makeup of a rock changes into a new substance when reacting to a chemical. Oxidation, hydrolysis, and acid rain are examples of chemical weathering.

Scientific Methods

How Science Works

Scientists make certain assumptions about nature that lead them to use the scientific method.

- The world can be understood through study and experimentation.
- The basic rules by which the universe works are the same everywhere.
- Scientific ideas can change. No matter how well one theory explains a set of observations, it is possible that another theory may fit just as well or better as our knowledge grows.
- Scientific knowledge is long-lasting. For example, calculations used to send people to the moon were based on Newton's laws, developed in the 1600s.
- There are many matters that cannot be examined in a scientific way, such as people's beliefs or issues of morality or religion. A hypothesis in these areas is not valid because it cannot be disproved.

Scientific Methods

Scientific methods are based on evidence instead of belief. They permit the acquisition of new scientific knowledge that is based on physical evidence. The essential elements of the scientific methods can be summarized in four steps—characterization of the subject of the investigation, which is accomplished by observation; the formulation of a hypothesis, which provides a casual explanation of the subject; the statement of a prediction that can be experimentally assessed; and the design of an experiment to test the hypothesis. The scientific process is iterative, which means that at any stage, scientists may repeat a part of the process. The results must also be verifiable, which means the results must be replicable by others.

Scientific Tools

Units of Measurement

It is important for students to understand that units of measurement, such as inches or meters, do not exist in nature. They are simply amounts that people have agreed to use as a standard so that they can communicate measurements and have someone else reproduce them.

- The earliest units of measurement were based on body parts. A cubit was the length of a person's forearm, from elbow to fingertip. A foot was the length of a man's foot. One problem was that men's arms and feet can vary in length by several inches!
- The Babylonians were the first to use a standard set of stones to measure weight. Other early cultures used wheat seeds and other grains as standards of weight and length.
- Roman soldiers kept track of the distance they traveled by counting paces.

Temperature and Temperature Scales

Temperature is a measure of how hot or cold something is. It should not be confused with heat, a form of energy that flows. Temperature can be measured on three scales: Fahrenheit, Celsius, and Kelvin. On the Fahrenheit scale, the temperature of boiling water is 212°F and of melting ice is 32°F. There are 180°F between them. On the Celsius scale, the temperature of boiling water is 100°C and of melting ice is 0°C. Each degree is one-hundredth of the difference between the two points on the scale. The Kelvin scale begins at the lowest theoretically possible temperature, which is called absolute zero, zero K, or zero Kelvins. This is the same as -273°C.

History of the Microscope

Magnifiers are mentioned in writings dating from the first century A.D. The earliest simple microscope, called a flea glass, was a tube with a plate for the object at one end and a lens at the other. Late in the sixteenth century, two Dutch spectacle makers developed the forerunner of the compound microscope and telescope. In 1609, Galileo made an instrument with a focusing device. The father of microscopy, Anton van Leeuwenhoek, of Holland, taught himself to grind and polish tiny lenses with great curvature that yielded magnifications. This led to his building microscopes and his famous biological discoveries. He was the first to see and describe bacteria, yeast cells, and to observe that a single drop of pond water is teeming with life.

Science Tools

Scales and balances are scientific tools used in homes as well as in scientific laboratories. A balance measures the mass of an object. The most basic tool for measuring mass is the pan balance. A pan balance uses a bar with a pan hanging from each end. At the center of the bar is a support, called a fulcrum, on which the bar can balance. The Egyptians used a balance of this type as early as 2500 B.C. Scales measure weight and other forces.

Simple Machines

Simple Machines

A simple machine is a device that makes work easier. There are six types of simple machines: the inclined plane, the wedge, the screw, the lever, the wheel-and-axle, and the pulley. All simple machines transfer force. Some change the direction of force, while others change the magnitude, or strength, of force. Still others change both the direction and the magnitude of force.

Most simple machines make work easier by allowing you to move things farther and/or faster. In these machines, a larger force is required, but over a shorter distance.

An inclined plane is really just a ramp, a flat surface that slopes. This type of simple machine is the only one that doesn't move. Instead, objects are moved over it in order to raise them. It takes less force to move an object up an inclined plane than it does to lift the object straight up. The trade-off is that the object must be moved a greater distance—the entire length of the inclined plane—to achieve the same height.

A wedge is an inclined plane that moves. Wedges are used to split or lift objects. Force is applied to the wide end of the wedge and gets transferred to the sides. In the process, the object either splits apart or gets lifted. It takes less force to drive a wedge into or under an object than it does to separate the object yourself. Cutting tools such as axes, scissor blades, saw blades, nail points, and plows are all examples of wedges.

A screw is an inclined plane wrapped around a cylinder. The spiral ridges around the shaft of the screw are called threads. As the screw is turned, the threads pull the object up the shaft. It takes less force to turn a screw than to pound a nail the same size. However, a screw must be turned many times, while a nail can be driven in just a few blows of a hammer.

A lever is a long rigid bar that rests on and pivots around a support called a fulcrum. Applying a force called the effort to one part of the lever causes the load at another place on the lever to move.

A wheel-and-axle is a simple machine that consists of a shaft, called the axle, inserted through the middle of a wheel. Any force that gets applied to the wheel gets transferred to the axle, and vice versa. A pulley is a wheel with a rope or chain wrapped around it. The wheel rotates around a fixed axle. The rope rides in a groove in the wheel. When the rope is pulled, the wheel turns.

Solar System

The Moon

Although students may think the moon and sun are the same size, the sun is really about 400 times the size of the moon. What we call moonlight is actually sunlight reflecting off the moon's surface. The moon itself has no light. We see half of the illuminated side of the moon when looking at a first-quarter or third-quarter moon. The first-quarter phase of the moon is labeled as such because it is one-quarter of the way through the lunar cycle. The third-quarter moon is three-quarters of the way through the cycle.

Satellites

An artificial, or human-made, satellite is any object placed into orbit around Earth and used for scientific and technological purposes. Most satellites are used for communication, military purposes, or scientific research. Scientific research satellites are used to explore Earth's atmosphere and space near Earth, to make images of Earth's surface or ocean floor, to track weather patterns, and to image astronomical objects without the interference of Earth's atmosphere. ***Sputnik 1***, launched by the Soviet Union on October 4, 1957, was the world's first artificial satellite. ***Sputnik 1*** was about the size of a basketball. Then on November 3, the Soviets launched a second satellite. It contained a small dog, named Laika. Three months later, the United States launched its first satellite, ***Explorer 1***. Today, many satellites orbit Earth. A balance between gravity and inertia makes this happen.

- The International Space Station, a satellite of Earth, is about 360 km (224 mi) above Earth's surface. It orbits Earth 16 times per day.
- The moon is a natural satellite of Earth; it is about 384,000 km (about 239,000 mi) from Earth and orbits Earth once every 27.3 days.

Sound

Loudness

The loudness of a sound refers to how strong the sound seems to people when they hear it. The intensity of a sound is determined by the amount of energy in the sound waves. Sound wave energy is less concentrated as it spreads outward in all directions from a source. As a result, the loudness of a sound decreases as the distance increases between the listener and the source of the sound. The word ***volume*** is also used to refer to the loudness of a sound.

Making Sound

All sounds—whether they are high or low, loud or soft—are made by a vibration. When an object vibrates, it causes the air around it to vibrate. The vibrations travel away from their point of origin in all directions. The vibrations can travel through gases, liquids, and solids. Humans produce sound in a section of the throat called the larynx. Two folds of tissue, called the vocal cords, cross the larynx. Between the vocal cords is an opening, or slit. When the vocal cords are relaxed, air rushes through the slit causing little or no vibration. When the vocal cords are tight, such as during speech, the rushing air causes the vocal cords to vibrate, which, in turn, causes sound. The tighter the vocal cords are, the faster the vibration and the higher pitched the sound is.

Sound Quality

Students may wonder why different musical instruments playing the same pitch sound different.

- The basic properties of sound are pitch, loudness, and quality. Sound "quality" is what allows the ear to distinguish between sounds.
- When an instrument plays a certain pitch, called the ***fundamental***, some parts of it also vibrate, producing different pitches called ***overtones***.
- The sound wave produced by the instrument is a complex combination of the fundamental tone and the overtones.
- When a sound wave reaches the ear, it creates an equally complex vibration of the eardrum. The person learns to associate the complex vibration with a particular instrument.

States of Matter

Physical Properties of Water

Water is the only common substance that exists in all three physical states under normal atmospheric conditions on Earth. However, its properties are not the same everywhere on Earth.

- At sea level, atmospheric pressure is 1 atmosphere (atm), and water boils at 100°C.
- At higher altitudes, atmospheric pressure is less than 1 atm, and liquid water boils at lower temperatures. For example, Twin Sisters Peak in Colorado's Rocky Mountain National Park is nearly 3,500 meters (11,450 feet) above sea level. Atmospheric pressure is about 0.65 atm, and water boils at 87°C. It takes almost twice as long to boil an egg at this elevation as at sea level.

Solubility of Gases

Solutions of gases in liquids are fairly common. All natural water contains dissolved oxygen (O_2) and nitrogen (N_2) along with other gases found in air. Carbonated beverages are solutions of carbon dioxide (CO_2) in water, along with sugar and flavoring. The solubility of a gas depends on its temperature and pressure.

- The gases dissolved in water become less soluble as the temperature increases. For example, at 30°C, the amount of dissolved O_2 in water is only about half of that found at 0°C. Fish depend on dissolved oxygen in water, and many of them cannot survive in warm water.
- The solubility of gases in water increases as the pressure increases. Carbonated beverages are bottled under pressure. When the cap is removed, the pressure drops and the solubility decreases, which accounts for the formation of bubbles.

Volcanoes

How Quickly Can a Mountain Form?

The natural processes to build a mountain are usually very slow. It takes hundreds of thousands of years for mountains ranges such as the Alps and the Rockies to form. Volcanic mountains can form very quickly, however. In early February 1943, the location where Paricutín Mountain (in Mexico) is now located was a flat cornfield. By the end of the month, a fissure had opened, and ash was accumulating. Within a year, that pile of ash was 335 m (1,100 ft) high. Within two years, the volcano had almost completely buried the village of Paricutín. Nine years later, when the volcanic eruption ended, Paricutín Mountain was about 425 m (1,400 ft) high and covered about 25 km^2 (10 mi^2).

Layers of Earth

The deepest hole ever drilled into the Earth's crust was only 12 km (7 mi) deep. To learn about deeper layers of Earth, scientists study lava from volcanoes as well as seismic waves produced by earthquakes. Waves travel at different speeds through different types of materials. These waves reveal that oceanic crust is on average about 6 km (3 mi) thick and continental crust is on average about 30 km (18 mi) thick. The crust and a small part of the mantle (collectively called the lithosphere) float on a soft, pliable portion of the mantle known as the asthenosphere. Magma is less dense than some material in the asthenosphere and in the crust, so it rises up through these layers and erupts on Earth's surface.

Predicting Volcanic Eruptions

Although it is not currently possible to predict exactly when a volcano will erupt, there are warning signs that sometimes indicate that an eruption may be imminent. As the magma in a volcano rises to the surface, there may be a series of small earthquakes. The rising magma may also cause the volcano to bulge, crack, or become distorted. The ground and any springs in the area may increase in temperature. These clues, unfortunately, can be unpredictable or misleading. Some or all of these events might continue to occur for days, weeks, months, or even years before the volcano actually erupts. Also, the pre-eruption events may occur and yet not be followed by an eruption.

Water

Point Pollution and Nonpoint Pollution

Point pollution and nonpoint pollution are the two ways that land and water are polluted.

- Point sources of pollution include discharge from oil spills, factory pipes, and sewage that flows directly from the source. These are more easily monitored than other kinds of pollution, because the source of the problem is often a pipe or another easily identifiable source.
- Nonpoint pollution is more dispersed. It's often more difficult to find the source and treat it. One example of nonpoint pollution is the runoff from farms that may include animal waste and pesticides sprayed onto field. Urban storm drains that collect water from rainstorms are another source of nonpoint pollution.

Water Cycle

The Water Cycle

Facts about the water cycle:

- People are part of the water cycle. A large percent of the human body is water. In fact, 75% of the brain is water!
- Earth contains the same amount of water today as it did when it first formed. Because water cycles continuously, the water you used to brush your teeth this morning could include water once used by dinosaurs.
- Water is one of the few substances that expands instead of shrinks when it freezes. Frozen water is less dense. This is why ice floats on liquid water.
- Only about 3% of Earth's water is fresh water (mostly ice); the rest is salt water.

Teacher Notes

Science Trade Books

Bibliography

Literature as Part of Science Instruction

This bibliography is a compilation of trade books listed for Grades 3-5. Many of these books are recommendations of The National Science Teachers Association (NSTA) and The Children's Book Council (CBC) as outstanding science trade books for children.

The panel has reviewed these books following rigorous selection criteria: they are of literary quality and contain substantial science content; the theories and facts are clearly distinguished; they are free of gender, ethnic, and socioeconomic bias; and they contain clear, accurate up-to-date information. Other selections are award-winning titles, or their authors have received awards.

As with all materials you share with your class, we suggest you review the books first to ensure their appropriateness. While titles are current at time of publication, they may go out of print without notice.

Grade 4

Actual Size by Steve Jenkins (Houghton Mifflin, 2004) invites readers to see how they measure up against a variety of different animals. Provides fun facts and physical dimensions of these critters. CHILDREN'S CHOICE; BOOKLIST EDITORS' CHOICE

Almost Invisible Irene by Daphne Skinner (Kane, 2003) tells the story of a shy girl who, after learning about animal camouflage, tries to avoid attracting attention to herself by blending in with her surroundings.

Animals by Miranda Smith (Kingfisher, 2009) provides vivid, three-dimensional illustrations that show a variety of animals in their natural habitats Students will discover how animals hunt, build their homes, and adapt to their surroundings.

Arctic Lights, Arctic Nights by Debbie S. Miller (Walker, 2007) portrays arctic animals and weather; each two-page spread features a different time of year, complete with the total number of sunlight hours and average daily temperatures. NSTA TRADE BOOK; OUTSTANDING SCIENCE TRADE BOOK

Brilliant Bees by Linda Glaser (Millbrook, 2003) describes the pollination process, hive structure and social order, methods of communication, and life cycle of the honeybee. NSTA TRADE BOOK; OUTSTANDING SCIENCE TRADE BOOK

Cell Division and Genetics by Robert Snedden (Heinemann, 2002) provides detailed information on the structure and function of cells. AWARD-WINNING AUTHOR

Claws, Coats and Camouflage: The Ways Animals Fit into Their World by Susan E. Goodman (Millbrook, 2001) poses questions that promote careful observations, critical analysis, and more inquiry into how well different animals, from insects to humans, are adapted for surviving in their environments. NSTA TRADE BOOK; OUTSTANDING SCIENCE TRADE BOOK

Dandelions: Stars in the Grass by Mia Posada (Carolrhoda, 2000) presents rhyming text with information about the dandelion, not as a weed, but as a flower of great beauty. Includes fun science activities to further engage young minds. NSTA TRADE BOOK; OUTSTANDING SCIENCE TRADE BOOK

Day Light, Night Light by Franklyn M. Branley (HarperCollins, 1975) discusses the properties of light, particularly its source in heat. AWARD-WINNING AUTHOR

Disgusting Plants by Connie Colwell Miller (Capstone, 2007) describes ten unusual plants and the characteristics that make them gross and disgusting.

Down Comes the Rain by Franklyn M. Branley (HarperCollins, 1997) explains the stages of the water cycle. AWARD-WINNING AUTHOR

Drip! Drop!: How Water Gets to Your Tap by Barbara Seuling (Holiday House, 2000) introduces students to JoJo and her dog Willy, who explain the water cycle and introduce fun experiments about filtration, evaporation, and condensation. AWARD-WINNING AUTHOR

Electrical Circuits: Harnessing Electricity by David Dreier (Compass Point, 2008) provides information about currents, how electricity works, and how circuits allow currents to flow in a continuous loop.

Energy by Christine Webster (Capstone, 2005) introduces the concept of energy and provides instructions for an activity to demonstrate some of its characteristics.

Energy by Don Herweck (Compass Point, 2009) describes the different forms of energy and how we use it in our everyday lives.

Find the Constellations by H.A. Rey (Houghton Mifflin, 2008) teaches readers how to recognize various constellations. Helpful charts and tables are provided in the back of the book. AWARD-WINNING AUTHOR AND ILLUSTRATOR

Flick a Switch: How Electricity Gets to Your Home by Barbara Seuling (Holiday House, 2003) describes how electricity was discovered, how early devices were invented to make use of it, and how it is generated in power plants and then distributed for many different uses. AWARD-WINNING AUTHOR

Flicker Flash by Joan Bransfield Graham (Houghton Mifflin, 1999) is a collection of poems celebrating light in its various forms, from candles and lamps to lightning and fireflies. NSTA TRADE BOOK; OUTSTANDING SCIENCE TRADE BOOK; SLJ BEST BOOK; NOTABLE CHILDREN'S BOOK IN THE LANGUAGE ARTS

Force and Motion: Laws of Movement by Don Nardo (Compass Point, 2008) focuses on English scientist Isaac Newton as well as his three laws of motion and how they govern the way we live. AWARD-WINNING AUTHOR

Forces and Motion: From Push to Shove by Christopher Cooper (Heinemann, 2003) discusses what happens when you push or pull an object and how forces can change the shape of an object. AWARD-WINNING AUTHOR

Forces: Science All Around Me by Karen Bryant-Mole (Heinemann, 2002) explains the basic principles of forces and movement through direct observation and through looking at everyday experiences.

From Seed to Daisy: Following the Life Cycle by Laura Purdie Salas (Picture Window, 2008) offers information about the Shasta daisy's life cycle from tiny seed to beautiful bloom.

Fully Charged: Electricity by Steve Parker (Heinemann, 2005) describes how electricity is generated, harnessed, and used, and explains the difference between electricity, including static electricity, and electrons. AWARD-WINNING AUTHOR

Girls Think of Everything: Stories of Ingenious Inventions by Women by Catherine Thimmesh (Houghton Mifflin, 2000) tells the story of how women throughout the ages have responded to situations confronting them in daily life by inventing various useful products. NSTA TRADE BOOK; OUTSTANDING SCIENCE TRADE BOOK; TEACHERS' CHOICE; SMITHSONIAN NOTABLE BOOK; IRA CHILDREN'S BOOK AWARD

Green Plants: From Roots to Leaves by Louise and Richard Spilsbury (Heinemann, 2004) provides information about the various parts of a plant via informational text and fun experiments and demonstrations.

Gulls . . . Gulls . . . Gulls by Gail Gibbons (Holiday House, 2001) uses detailed text and clear illustrations to describe nearly every aspect of gulls, from their appearance to migration and more. NSTA TRADE BOOK; OUTSTANDING SCIENCE TRADE BOOK

A History of Super Science: Atoms and Elements by Andrew Solway (Raintree, 2006) offers a basic introduction to atoms, elements, and various other components of chemistry, including the Periodic Table and famous alchemists.

Hot and Cold by Karen Bryant-Mole (Heinemann, 2002) introduces the scientific properties of heat and cold, examining such topics as temperature, thermometers, freezing, and melting.

If You Find a Rock by Peggy Christian (Harcourt, 2000) celebrates the variety of rocks, including skipping rocks, chalk rocks, and splashing rocks. NOTABLE CHILDREN'S BOOK IN THE LANGUAGE ARTS

Inventions by Glenn Murphy (Simon & Schuster, 2009) brings inventions to life with state-of-the-art, three-dimensional illustrations and informational text about inventions through the years—from prehistoric times up until today.

Jane Goodall: Legendary Primatologist by Brenda Haugen (Compass Point, 2006) tells the story of Jane Goodall, her research on chimpanzee behavior, and how she went on to found a conservation organization to improve the environment for all living things.

Life Processes: From Reproduction to Respiration by Louise and Richard Spilsbury (Heinemann, 2004) describes the processes by which living things abide in order to thrive and survive.

Light and Sound by Dr. Mike Goldsmith (Kingfisher, 2007) takes students on a journey of discovery as they learn how light is made, how light makes electricity, and how sound travels.

Light: From Sun to Bulbs by Christopher Cooper (Heinemann, 2003) invites students to investigate the dazzling world of physical science and light through fun experiments. AWARD-WINNING AUTHOR

Light: Look Out! by Wendy Sadler (Raintree, 2006) enlightens readers about the way light is present in their everyday lives. Offers information about color, reflection, and electricity.

Lightning by Seymour Simon (Collins, 2006) uses spectacular photos to introduce readers to the forms of lightning, to streamers called stepped leaders, and to the main lightning bolt itself. NSTA TRADE BOOK; OUTSTANDING SCIENCE TRADE BOOK; CHILDREN'S CHOICE

A Log's Life by Wendy Pfeffer (Aladdin, 2007) introduces readers to the life cycle of a tree and explains how animals depend on the tree for food and shelter, as well as how animals assist in the decay process. NSTA TRADE BOOK; OUTSTANDING SCIENCE TRADE BOOK

Matter by Jane Weir (Compass Point, 2009) explores the different states of matter, the elements of the Periodic Table, and atoms—the smallest particles that make up elements.

Matter by Mir Tamim Ansary (Heinemann, 2002) looks at the physical world and the properties and behavior of different kinds of matter.

A Matter of Survival: Properties of Matter by Ann Weil (Raintree, 2006) provides information about the states of matter as well as mass, density, volume, buoyancy, and the physical and chemical changes of matter. AWARD-WINNING AUTHOR

The Moon by Seymour Simon (Simon & Schuster, 2003) tells about the work of early scientists and takes the reader through the moon explorations of the Apollo astronauts. NSTA TRADE BOOK; OUTSTANDING SCIENCE TRADE BOOK; ALA NOTABLE BOOK

Muscles: Our Muscular System by Seymour Simon (HarperCollins, 2000) takes the reader on a tour through the human muscular systems, explaining the different types of muscles and their functions and purposes, and the effects that exercise has on muscles. NSTA TRADE BOOK; OUTSTANDING SCIENCE TRADE BOOK

My Light by Molly Bang (Blue Sky, 2004) is told from the sun's point of view and describes how various forms of energy are derived from the heat and light of the sun. ALA NOTABLE BOOK

Neo Leo: The Ageless Ideas of Leonardo da Vinci by Gene Barretta (Henry Holt, 2009) tells the story of artist, inventor, engineer, and scientist Leonardo da Vinci, accompanied by brightly colored illustrations. AWARD-WINNING AUTHOR

Next Stop Neptune: Experiencing the Solar System by Alvin Jenkins (Houghton Mifflin, 2004) takes readers on a virtual tour of our solar system, providing fun facts about planets, moons, and asteroids.

Night Wonders by Jane Ann Peddicord (Charlesbridge, 2005) takes readers on a journey through space, providing information about stars, the sun and moon, planets, nebulae, and galaxies. IRA CHILDREN'S BOOK AWARD

Oak Tree by Gordon Morrison (Houghton Mifflin, 2000) describes the impact of the changing seasons on an old oak tree and the life that surrounds it. AWARD-WINNING AUTHOR

One Giant Leap: The Story of Neil Armstrong by Don Brown (Houghton Mifflin, 1998) discusses the life and accomplishments of astronaut Neil Armstrong, from his childhood in Ohio to his famous moon landing. PARENTS' CHOICE

One Tiny Turtle by Nicola Davies (Walker, 2008) describes the life cycle of the loggerhead sea turtle. TEACHERS' CHOICE

Physics: Why Matter Matters! by Dan Green (Kingfisher, 2008) combines science and art to bring the world of physics to life with fun and wacky characters to explain the building blocks of our universe.

Postcards from Pluto: A Tour of the Solar System by Loreen Leedy (Holiday House, 2006) offers readers a virtual tour of the solar system, describing each planet. BOOKLIST EDITORS' CHOICE

Pumpkin Circle: The Story of a Garden by George Levenson (Tricycle, 2004) captures each phase of the pumpkin's life cycle with time-lapse photography: seeds sprouting, flowers blooming, bees buzzing, pumpkins growing, and finally, a pumpkin returning to the earth. NSTA TRADE BOOK; OUTSTANDING SCIENCE TRADE BOOK

Rachel: The Story of Rachel Carson by Amy Ehrlich (Silver Whistle, 2003) describes the life and work of pioneer nature writer and activist Rachel Carson, who was a leader in the environmental movement. NSTA TRADE BOOK; OUTSTANDING SCIENCE TRADE BOOK; NOTABLE SOCIAL STUDIES TRADE BOOK

Raptors, Fossils, Fins, and Fangs by Brad Matsen and Ray Troll (Tricycle, 2004) introduces lesser-known prehistoric creatures, including the giant sea scorpion called eurypterid, the Helicoprion shark, and the carnivorous land dinosaur Deinonychus.

Saving Birds: Heroes Around the World by Pete Salmansohn and Stephen W. Kress (Tilbury House, 2005) features fascinating stories of six bird species that were saved from extinction with the help of naturalists, residents, and community leaders. NSTA TRADE BOOK; OUTSTANDING SCIENCE TRADE BOOK

Sea Clocks: The Story of Longitude by Louise Borden (Margaret K. McElderry, 2004) tells the story of Englishman John Harrison who, with no scientific training, worked tirelessly for more than forty years to create an accurate clock. AWARD-WINNING AUTHOR

Seeing by Mary Mackill (Heinemann, 2006) provides information on the sense of sight, the parts of the eye, how we see, and tools that can help us see.

Slugs by Anthony D. Fredericks (Lerner, 2000) describes the physical characteristics, habitat, and behavior of these slimy creatures that spend their lives crawling on their stomachs. NSTA TRADE BOOK; OUTSTANDING SCIENCE TRADE BOOK

Snowflake Bentley by Jacqueline Briggs Martin (Houghton Mifflin, 1998) is the story of Wilson "Snowflake" Bentley, a self-taught scientist and photographer, who developed a technique to photograph snowflakes. NSTA TRADE BOOK; OUTSTANDING SCIENCE TRADE BOOK; ALA NOTABLE BOOK; BOOKLIST EDITORS' CHOICE

Solar Power by Josepha Sherman (Capstone, 2004) introduces the history, uses, production, advantages and disadvantages, and future of solar energy as a power resource.

The Stars by Patricia Whitehouse (Heinemann, 2004) provides information about stars, including star nurseries, star energy, star color and temperature, and twinkling. Combines information text with stunning photographs.

States of Matter: A Question and Answer Book by Fiona Bayrock (Capstone, 2006) explores the composition of matter, its changing states, and the effects of changing between states.

Summer Ice: Life Along the Antarctic Peninsula by Bruce McMillan (Houghton Mifflin, 1995) informs readers about the coldest continent and how, despite its frigid temperatures, various plants and animals can survive there. NSTA TRADE BOOK; OUTSTANDING SCIENCE TRADE BOOK

Sun by Steve Tomecek (National Geographic Society, 2006) describes the physics and characteristics of the sun. AWARD-WINNING AUTHOR

Temperature by Rebecca Olien (Capstone, 2005) introduces the concept of temperature and provides instructions for an activity to demonstrate some of its characteristics.

The Top of the World: Climbing Mount Everest by Steve Jenkins (Houghton Mifflin, 1999) describes the conditions and terrain of Mount Everest, attempts that have been made to scale this peak, and information about the equipment and techniques of mountain climbing. ALA NOTABLE BOOK; SLJ BEST BOOK; BOSTON GLOBE - HORN BOOK AWARD; ORBIS PICTUS HONOR

Tornadoes by Seymour Simon (HarperCollins, 2001) explains where and how tornadoes develop, how they are tracked, and the dangers associated with them. NSTA TRADE BOOK; OUTSTANDING SCIENCE TRADE BOOK

Under Pressure: Forces by Ann Fullick (Heinemann, 2005) provides an overview of what forces are and how they affect the way we live, describing such forces as gravity, pressure, balanced and unbalanced forces, and motion on a curve.

Water Dance by Thomas Locker (Voyager/Harcourt, 2002) involves readers in a question-and-answer format, observing the natural movement of water. NSTA TRADE BOOK; OUTSTANDING SCIENCE TRADE BOOK; TEACHERS' CHOICE; NOTABLE CHILDREN'S BOOK IN THE LANGUAGE ARTS

Weather Patterns by Monica Hughes (Heinemann, 2004) describes different types of climate in various places and the weather that occurs during the seasons. AWARD-WINNING AUTHOR

What Do You Do When Something Wants to Eat You? by Steve Jenkins (Houghton Mifflin, 1997) introduces young readers to the specialized adaptations animals use to avoid the constant threat of becoming another animal's meal. NSTA TRADE BOOK; OUTSTANDING SCIENCE TRADE BOOK; BOOKLIST EDITORS' CHOICE

What's the Matter in Mr. Whiskers' Room? by Michael Elsohn Ross (Candlewick, 2007) tells the story of a teacher who encourages his students to be scientists as they explore matter through an array of hands-on exploration experiments. AWARD-WINNING AUTHOR

Your Bones by Terri DeGezelle (Bridgestone, 2002) introduces bones, their makeup and function, and bone diseases, and ways to keep bones healthy.

COMMON CORE

ENGLISH LANGUAGE ARTS

Correlation

Correlations to the Common Core State Standards for English Language Arts are provided on these pages.

Grade 4 Standard Code	Descriptor	Teacher Edition Page Citations
Range of Reading and Level of Text Complexity		
RL.4.10	By the end of the year, read and comprehend literature, including stories, dramas, and poetry, in the grades 4–5 text complexity band proficiently, with scaffolding as needed at the high end of the range.	See the Science Trade Books Bibliography on pp. PG68–PG71 for some suggested titles.
Reading Standards for Informational Text		
Key Ideas and Details		
RI.4.1	Refer to details and examples in a text when explaining what the text says explicitly and when drawing inferences from the text.	5, 7, 9, 11, 13, 19, 21, 23, 29, 31, 33, 35, 37, 47, 49, 51, 65, 67, 69, 71, 81, 83, 85, 87, 89, 105, 107, 109, 111, 119, 121, 123, 125, 127, 137, 139, 141, 143, 145, 175, 177, 179, 181, 183, 191, 193, 195, 197, 199, 209, 211, 213, 215, 217, 223, 225, 227, 229, 247, 249, 251, 253, 261, 263, 265, 267, 269, 275, 277, 279, 281, 289, 299, 301, 303, 305, 307, 317, 319, 321, 329, 331, 333, 335, 337, 351, 353, 354, 355, 357, 359, 361, 375, 377, 379, 393, 395, 397, 399, 407, 409, 411, 413, 431, 433, 435, 437, 439, 449, 451, 453, 465, 467, 469, 485, 487, 489, 491, 503, 505, 507, 509, 519, 521, 523, 525, 539, 541, 543, 545, 547

Grade 4 Standard Code	Descriptor	Teacher Edition Page Citations
RI.4.2	Determine the main idea of a text and explain how it is supported by key details; summarize the text.	Use the Summarize Ideas sections to provide opportunities for students to summarize concepts. For example, see pages 5, 7, 9, 11, 13, 19, 21, 23, 29, 31, 33, 35, 37, 47, 49, 51, 65, 67, 69, 71, 81, 83, 85, 86, 87, 89, 105, 107, 109, 111, 119, 121, 123, 125, 127, 137, 139, 141, 143, 145, 175, 177, 179, 181, 183, 191, 193, 195, 197, 199, 209, 211, 213, 215, 217, 223, 225, 227, 229, 247, 249, 251, 253, 260, 261, 263, 265, 267, 269, 270, 275, 277, 278–279, 282, 289, 299, 301, 303, 305, 307, 317, 319, 321, 329, 331, 333, 335, 337, 353, 355, 357, 358, 359, 361, 375, 377, 379, 431, 433, 435, 437, 439, 449, 451, 453, 465, 467, 469, 539, 541, 543, 545, 547
RI.4.3	Explain events, procedures, ideas, or concepts in a historical, scientific, or technical text, including what happened and why, based on specific information in the text.	5, 7, 9, 11, 13, 19, 21, 23, 29, 31, 33, 35, 37, 47, 49, 51, 65, 67, 69, 71, 81, 83, 85, 86, 87, 89, 105, 107, 109, 111, 119, 121, 123, 125, 127, 137, 139, 141, 143, 145, 175, 177, 179, 181, 183, 191, 193, 195, 197, 199, 209, 211, 213, 215, 217, 223, 225, 227, 229, 247, 249, 251, 253, 260, 261, 263, 265, 267, 269, 270, 275, 277, 278–279, 282, 289, 299, 301, 303, 305, 307, 317, 319, 321, 329, 331, 333, 335, 337, 353, 355, 357, 358, 359, 361, 375, 377, 379, 431, 433, 435, 437, 439, 449, 451, 453, 465, 467, 469, 539, 541, 543, 545, 547

Grade 4 Standard Code	Descriptor	Teacher Edition Page Citations
Craft and Structure		
RI.4.4	Determine the meaning of general academic and domain-specific words or phrases in a text relevant to a grade 4 topic or subject area.	Use the strategies in the Develop Science Vocabulary entries in the side margins of the Teacher Edition. Use the Interactive Glossary with every lesson.
RI.4.5	Describe the overall structure (e.g., chronology, comparison, cause/effect, problem/solution) of events, ideas, concepts, or information in a text or part of a text.	4, 6, 8, 10, 12, 18, 20, 22, 28, 30, 32, 34, 36, 46, 48, 50, 70, 80–81, 82, 84, 86, 88, 104, 106, 108, 110, 118, 120, 122, 124, 126, 136, 138, 140, 142, 144, 167A, 174, 176, 178, 180, 182, 190, 191, 192, 194, 196, 198, 208, 210, 212, 214, 216, 222, 224, 226, 228, 246, 248, 250, 252, 260, 262–263, 264, 266, 268, 274, 276, 278, 280, 298, 300, 302, 304, 306, 316, 318, 320, 328, 330, 332, 334, 336, 352, 354, 356, 358, 360, 374, 376, 378, 392, 394, 396, 398, 406, 408, 410, 412, 430, 432, 434, 436, 438, 448, 450, 452, 464, 466, 468, 484, 486, 488, 490, 502, 504, 506, 508, 518, 520, 522, 524, 538, 540, 542, 544, 546
Integration of Knowledge and Ideas		
RI.4.7	Interpret information presented visually, orally, or quantitatively (e.g., in charts, graphs, diagrams, time lines, animations, or interactive elements on Web pages) and explain how the information contributes to an understanding of the text in which it appears.	Use the strategies in the Interpret Visuals entries in the side margins of the Teacher Edition.
RI.4.9	Integrate information from two texts on the same topic in order to write or speak about the subject knowledgeably.	Texts with topics related to the Student Edition can be found in the Leveled Readers.

Grade 4 Standard Code	Descriptor	Teacher Edition Page Citations
Range of Reading and Level of Text Complexity		
RI.4.10	By the end of year, read and comprehend informational texts, including history/social studies, science, and technical texts, in the grades 4–5 text complexity band proficiently, with scaffolding as needed at the high end of the range.	See the Science Trade Books Bibliography on pp. PG68–PG71 for some suggested titles.
Reading Standards: Foundational Skills		
Phonics and Word Recognition		
RF.4.3	Know and apply grade-level phonics and word analysis skills in decoding words.	
RF.4.3.a	Use combined knowledge of all letter-sound correspondences, syllabication patterns, and morphology (e.g., roots and affixes) to read accurately unfamiliar multisyllabic words in context and out of context.	87, 109, 110, 154, 181, 190, 209, 321, 374, 466, 508, 520
Fluency		
RF.4.4	Read with sufficient accuracy and fluency to support comprehension.	
RF.4.4.a	Read on-level text with purpose and understanding.	Reproducible student worksheets addressing oral reading fluency are provided with each Leveled Reader Teacher Guide.
RF.4.4.b	Read on-level prose and poetry orally with accuracy, appropriate rate, and expression on successive readings.	135
Writing Standards		
Text Types and Purposes		
W.4.1	Write opinion pieces on topics or texts, supporting a point of view with reasons and information.	
W.4.1.a	Introduce a topic or text clearly, state an opinion, and create an organizational structure in which related ideas are grouped to support the writer's purpose.	51, 227, 229, 234A, 366A, 397, 410, 467, 507
W.4.1.b	Provide reasons that are supported by facts and details.	51, 227, 229, 366A, 397, 410, 467, 507
W.4.1.d	Provide a concluding statement or section related to the opinion presented.	51, 227, 229, 234A, 366A, 397, 410, 467, 507
W.4.2	Write informative/explanatory texts to examine a topic and convey ideas and information clearly.	

Grade 4 Standard Code	Descriptor	Teacher Edition Page Citations
W.4.2.a	Introduce a topic clearly and group related information in paragraphs and sections; include formatting (e.g., headings), illustrations, and multimedia when useful to aiding comprehension.	7, 20, 26A, 29, 40A, 71, 76A, 92A, 111, 120, 134A, 136, 150, 177, 188A, 213, 215, 235, 284A, 305, 312A, 337, 340A, 366A, 375, 402A, 407, 412, 416A, 421, 436, 458A, 529
W.4.2.b	Develop the topic with facts, definitions, concrete details, quotations, or other information and examples related to the topic.	7, 20, 26A, 54A, 71, 76A, 92A, 111, 120, 134A, 136, 150, 152, 177, 188A, 204A, 213, 215, 232A, 235, 284A, 305, 337, 340A, 366A, 375, 402A, 416A, 421, 436, 529
W.4.2.c	Link ideas within categories of information using words and phrases (e.g., another, for example, also, because).	71, 76A, 92A, 136, 150, 177, 188A, 215, 220A, 235, 305, 421, 529
W.4.2.d	Use precise language and domain-specific vocabulary to inform about or explain the topic.	7, 20, 26A, 71, 76A, 92A, 106, 107, 111, 120, 132A, 136, 150, 152, 177, 188A, 204A, 213, 215, 220A, 232A, 235, 284A, 305, 337, 340A, 366A, 375, 402A, 407, 412, 416A, 421, 436, 458A, 514A, 529
W.4.2.e	Provide a concluding statement or section related to the information or explanation presented.	7, 20, 71, 76A, 92A, 120, 134A, 136, 150, 188A, 215, 232A, 235, 284A, 305, 337, 366A, 375, 402A, 416A, 421, 436, 514A, 529
W.4.3	Write narratives to develop real or imagined experiences or events using effective technique, descriptive details, and clear event sequences.	
W.4.3.a	Orient the reader by establishing a situation and introducing a narrator and/or characters; organize an event sequence that unfolds naturally.	82, 86, 114A, 124, 132A, 159, 164A, 177, 195, 220A, 265, 272A, 281, 340A, 355, 382A, 412, 449, 523, 528A, 545
W.4.3.b	Use dialogue and description to develop experiences and events or show the responses of characters to situations.	82, 107, 114A, 124, 132A, 159, 161, 164A, 177, 195, 265, 272A, 281, 340A, 382A, 412, 449, 523, 528A, 545
W.4.3.c	Use a variety of transitional words and phrases to manage the sequence of events.	82, 124, 132A, 177, 195, 272A, 281, 523, 528A
W.4.3.d	Use concrete words and phrases and sensory details to convey experiences and events precisely.	82, 86, 107, 114A, 124, 132A, 159, 164A, 177, 195, 220A, 248, 265, 272A, 281, 319, 340A, 355, 382A, 397, 412, 449, 523, 528A, 545

Grade 4 Standard Code	Descriptor	Teacher Edition Page Citations
W.4.3.e	Provide a conclusion that follows from the narrated experiences or events.	82, 86, 114A, 124, 159, 177, 195, 265, 272A, 281, 340A, 382A, 412, 523, 528A, 545
Production and Distribution of Writing		
W.4.4	Produce clear and coherent writing in which the development and organization are appropriate to task, purpose, and audience. (Grade-specific expectations for writing types are defined in standards 1–3 above.)	7, 20, 26A, 40A, 51, 54A, 71, 76A, 82, 86, 92A, 107, 110, 114A, 120, 124, 132A, 136, 150, 177, 188A, 195, 204A, 213, 215, 220A, 227, 229, 232A, 234A, 235, 248, 265, 272A, 281, 284A, 305, 312A, 319, 337, 340A, 355, 366A, 375, 382A, 402A, 407, 412, 416A, 421, 436, 449, 458A, 507, 514A, 523, 528A, 529, 545
W.4.6	With some guidance and support from adults, use technology, including the Internet, to produce and publish writing as well as to interact and collaborate with others; demonstrate sufficient command of keyboarding skills to type a minimum of one page in a single sitting.	The Go Digital Path allows students to use digital tools to present a topic.
Research to Build and Present Knowledge		
W.4.7	Conduct short research projects that build knowledge through investigation of different aspects of a topic.	76A, 92A, 114A, 132A, 136, 150, 161, 164A, 188A, 204A, 213, 215, 227, 232A, 234A, 272A, 305, 312A, 340A, 402A
W.4.8	Recall relevant information from experiences or gather relevant information from print and digital sources; take notes and categorize information, and provide a list of sources.	76A, 82, 114, 120, 132A, 136, 150, 161, 188A, 204A, 213, 258A, 312A, 324A, 340A, 444A, 458A, 472A, 528A
W.4.9	Draw evidence from literary or informational texts to support analysis, reflection, and research.	
W.4.9.b	Apply grade 4 Reading standards to informational texts (e.g., "Explain how an author uses reasons and evidence to support particular points in a text").	235
Range of Writing		
W.4.10	Write routinely over extended time frames (time for research, reflection, and revision) and shorter time frames (a single sitting or a day or two) for a range of discipline-specific tasks, purposes, and audiences.	528A

Grade 4 Standard Code	Descriptor	Teacher Edition Page Citations
Speaking and Listening Standards		
Comprehension and Collaboration		
SL.4.1	Engage effectively in a range of collaborative discussions (one-on-one, in groups, and teacher-led) with diverse partners on grade 4 topics and texts, building on others' ideas and expressing their own clearly.	
SL.4.1.a	Come to discussions prepared, having read or studied required material; explicitly draw on that preparation and other information known about the topic to explore ideas under discussion.	Use the Generate Ideas sections to access prior knowledge and to provide opportunities for students to discuss their own ideas about a topic. For example, see pages 4, 6, 8, 10, 12, 18, 20, 22, 28, 30, 32, 34, 36, 46, 48, 50, 64, 66, 68, 70, 80, 82, 84, 86, 104, 106, 108, 110, 118, 120, 122, 124, 126, 136, 138, 140, 142, 144, 174, 176, 178, 180, 182, 190, 192, 194, 196, 198, 208, 210, 212, 214, 216, 222, 224, 226, 228, 246, 248, 250, 252, 260, 262, 264, 266, 268, 274, 276, 278, 280, 298, 300, 302, 304, 306, 316, 318, 320, 328, 330, 332, 334, 336, 352, 354, 356, 358, 360, 374, 376, 378, 392, 394, 396, 398, 406, 408, 410, 412, 430, 432, 434, 436, 438, 448, 450, 452, 464, 466, 468, 484, 486, 488, 490, 502, 504, 506, 508, 518, 520, 522, 524, 538, 540, 542, 544, 546
SL.4.1.b	Follow agreed-upon rules for discussions and carry out assigned roles.	104, 106, 108, 109, 110, 164A, 333, 324A, 430

Grade 4 Standard Code	Descriptor	Teacher Edition Page Citations
SL.4.1.c	Pose and respond to specific questions to clarify or follow up on information, and make comments that contribute to the discussion and link to the remarks of others.	4, 6, 8, 10, 12, 18, 20, 22, 28, 30, 32, 34, 36, 46, 48, 50, 64, 66, 68, 70, 80, 82, 84, 86, 104, 106, 108, 110, 118, 120, 122, 124, 126, 136, 138, 140, 142, 144, 174, 176, 178, 180, 182, 190, 192, 194, 196, 198, 208, 210, 212, 214, 216, 222, 224, 226, 228, 246, 248, 250, 252, 260, 262, 264, 266, 268, 274, 276, 278, 280, 298, 300, 302, 304, 306, 316, 318, 320, 324A 328, 330, 332, 334, 336, 352, 354, 356, 358, 360, 374, 376, 378, 392, 394, 396, 398, 406, 408, 410, 412, 430, 432, 434, 436, 438, 448, 450, 452, 464, 466, 468, 538, 540, 542, 544, 546
SL.4.1.d	Review the key ideas expressed and explain their own ideas and understanding in light of the discussion.	5, 7, 9, 11, 13, 19, 21, 23, 29, 31, 33, 35, 37, 47, 49, 51, 65, 67, 69, 71, 81, 83, 85, 86, 87, 89, 105, 107, 109, 111, 119, 121, 123, 125, 127, 137, 139, 141, 143, 145, 175, 177, 179, 181, 183, 191, 193, 195, 197, 199, 209, 211, 213, 215, 217, 223, 225, 227, 229, 247, 249, 251, 253, 260, 261, 263, 265, 267, 269, 270, 275, 277, 278–279, 282, 289, 299, 301, 303, 305, 307, 317, 319, 321, 329, 331, 333, 335, 337, 353, 355, 357, 358, 359, 361, 375, 377, 379, 431, 433, 435, 437, 439, 449, 451, 453, 465, 467, 469, 539, 541, 543, 545, 547
Presentation of Knowledge and Ideas		
SL.4.4	Report on a topic or text, tell a story, or recount an experience in an organized manner, using appropriate facts and relevant, descriptive details to support main ideas or themes; speak clearly at an understandable pace.	76A, 178, 215, 324A, 402A, 436

Grade 4 Standard Code	Descriptor	Teacher Edition Page Citations
Language Standards		
Conventions of Standard English		
L.4.1	Demonstrate command of the conventions of standard English grammar and usage when writing or speaking.	
L.4.1.f	Produce complete sentences, recognizing and correcting inappropriate fragments and run-ons.	407
L.4.1.g	Correctly use frequently confused words (e.g., to, too, two; there, their).	158
L.4.2	Demonstrate command of the conventions of standard English capitalization, punctuation, and spelling when writing.	
L.4.2.d	Spell grade-appropriate words correctly, consulting references as needed.	194, 381, 455, 471
Knowledge of Language		
L.4.3	Use knowledge of language and its conventions when writing, speaking, reading, or listening.	
L.4.3.a	Choose words and phrases to convey ideas precisely.	123, 174, 178, 398, 406, 409, 447, 520, 522, 523, 528A
L.4.3.b	Choose punctuation for effect.	125
Vocabulary Acquisition and Use		
L.4.4	Determine or clarify the meaning of unknown and multiple-meaning words and phrases based on grade 4 reading and content, choosing flexibly from an array of strategies.	
L.4.4.a	Use context (e.g., definitions, examples, or restatements in text) as a clue to the meaning of a word or phrase.	34, 66, 84, 174, 193, 194, 209, 210, 218, 246, 251, 298, 317, 331, 352, 374, 392, 395, 406, 409, 430, 454, 504, 505
L.4.4.b	Use common, grade-appropriate Greek and Latin affixes and roots as clues to the meaning of a word (e.g., telegraph, photograph, autograph).	67, 110, 502, 514A, 520, 522, 524
L.4.4.c	Consult reference materials (e.g., dictionaries, glossaries, thesauruses), both print and digital, to find the pronunciation and determine or clarify the precise meaning of key words and phrases.	The Vocabulary and Interactive Glossary feature allows students to use digital glossaries to add notes, illustrations, and sentences to vocabulary words.
L.4.5	Demonstrate understanding of figurative language, word relationships, and nuances in word meanings.	
L.4.5.b	Recognize and explain the meaning of common idioms, adages, and proverbs.	378, 451, 540

Grade 4 Standard Code	Descriptor	Teacher Edition Page Citations
L.4.5.c	Demonstrate understanding of words by relating them to their opposites (antonyms) and to words with similar but not identical meanings (synonyms).	4, 8, 174, 210, 224, 226, 398, 520
L.4.6	Acquire and use accurately grade-appropriate general academic and domain-specific words and phrases, including those that signal precise actions, emotions, or states of being (e.g., quizzed, whined, stammered) and that are basic to a particular topic (e.g., wildlife, conservation, and endangered when discussing animal preservation).	1L–1M, 5, 7, 9, 19, 31, 33, 35, 47, 49, 61J–61K, 65, 67, 81, 101L–101M, 107, 108, 110, 118, 120, 122, 126, 142, 143, 146, 147, 152, 154, 159, 171L–171M, 175, 176, 179, 181, 190, 191, 193, 197, 200, 201, 209, 210, 219, 227, 228, 243J–243K, 247, 249, 251, 261, 269, 274, 276, 279, 295L–295M, 299, 300, 305, 319, 328, 349J–349K, 353, 356, 359, 374, 375, 378, 389J–389K, 393, 397, 407, 409, 411, 427J–427K, 431, 433, 437, 449, 451, 453, 455, 464, 465, 467, 470, 471, 481J–481K, 487, 490, 502, 504, 507, 519, 520, 522, 523, 524, 525, 528A, 535H–535I, 539, 542, 544

COMMON CORE

MATHEMATICS CORRELATION

Correlations to the Common Core State Standards for Mathematics are provided on these pages.

Grade 4 Standard Code	Descriptor	Teacher Edition Page Citations
Mathematical Practices		
4.MP.1	Make sense of problems and persevere in solving them.	23, 119, 139, 307, 320, 325, 434, 469, 509, 514A, 528A
4.MP.2	Reason abstractly and quantitatively.	199
4.MP.4	Model with mathematics.	11, 16A, 23, 123, 132A, 164A, 176, 198, 199, 204A, 217, 232A, 312A, 320, 340A, 357, 394, 397, 408
4.MP.5	Use appropriate tools strategically.	35, 49, 357, 394, 449
4.MP.6	Attend to precision.	23, 137, 211, 357, 397, 449, 509, 514A
4.MP.7	Look for and make use of structure.	176
4.MP.8	Look for and express regularity in repeated reasoning.	319, 509, 514A
Operations and Algebraic Thinking		
Use the four operations with whole numbers to solve problems.		
4.OA.2	Multiply or divide to solve word problems involving multiplicative comparison, e.g., by using drawings and equations with a symbol for the unknown number to represent the problem, distinguishing multiplicative comparison from additive comparison.	249, 528A
4.OA.3	Solve multistep word problems posed with whole numbers and having whole-number answers using the four operations, including problems in which remainders must be interpreted. Represent these problems using equations with a letter standing for the unknown quantity. Assess the reasonableness of answers using mental computation and estimation strategies including rounding.	182, 188A, 214, 223, 227, 328, 528A
Gain familiarity with factors and multiples.		
4.OA.4	Find all factor pairs for a whole number in the range 1–100. Recognize that a whole number is a multiple of each of its factors. Determine whether a given whole number in the range 1–100 is a multiple of a given one-digit number. Determine whether a given whole number in the range 1–100 is prime or composite.	253

Grade 4 Standard Code	Descriptor	Teacher Edition Page Citations
Generate and analyze patterns.		
4.OA.5	Generate a number or shape pattern that follows a given rule. Identify apparent features of the pattern that were not explicit in the rule itself. *For example, given the rule "Add 3" and the starting number 1, generate terms in the resulting sequence and observe that the terms appear to alternate between odd and even numbers. Explain informally why the numbers will continue to alternate in this way.*	153, 514A
Number and Operations in Base Ten		
Generalize place value understanding for multi-digit whole numbers.		
4.NBT.1	Recognize that in a multi-digit whole number, a digit in one place represents ten times what it represents in the place to its right. *For example, recognize that 700 ÷ 70 = 10 by applying concepts of place value and division.*	253
Use place value understanding and properties of operations to perform multi-digit arithmetic.		
4.NBT.4	Fluently add and subtract multi-digit whole numbers using the standard algorithm.	26A, 33, 36, 87, 127, 263, 281, 284, 298, 328
4.NBT.5	Multiply a whole number of up to four digits by a one-digit whole number, and multiply two two-digit numbers, using strategies based on place value and the properties of operations. Illustrate and explain the calculation by using equations, rectangular arrays, and/or area models.	83, 87, 127, 227, 253, 258A, 458A, 472A, 542
4.NBT.6	Find whole-number quotients and remainders with up to four-digit dividends and one-digit divisors, using strategies based on place value, the properties of operations, and/or the relationship between multiplication and division. Illustrate and explain the calculation by using equations, rectangular arrays, and/or area models.	48, 214, 249, 284, 320, 458A, 543
Number and Operations—Fractions		
Extend understanding of fraction equivalence and ordering.		
4.NF.1	Explain why a fraction a/b is equivalent to a fraction $(n \times a)/(n \times b)$ by using visual fraction models, with attention to how the number and size of the parts differ even though the two fractions themselves are the same size. Use this principle to recognize and generate equivalent fractions.	49, 68, 123, 413
4.NF.2	Compare two fractions with different numerators and different denominators, e.g., by creating common denominators or numerators, or by comparing to a benchmark fraction such as 1/2. Recognize that comparisons are valid only when the two fractions refer to the same whole. Record the results of comparisons with symbols >, =, or <, and justify the conclusions, e.g., by using a visual fraction model.	413

Grade 4 Standard Code	Descriptor	Teacher Edition Page Citations
Build fractions from unit fractions by applying and extending previous understandings of operations on whole numbers.		
4.NF.3	3. Understand a fraction a/b with $a > 1$ as a sum of fractions $1/b$. a. Understand addition and subtraction of fractions as joining and separating parts referring to the same whole. b. Decompose a fraction into a sum of fractions with the same denominator in more than one way, recording each decomposition by an equation. Justify decompositions, e.g., by using a visual fraction model. *Examples:* $3/8 = 1/8 + 1/8 + 1/8$; $3/8 = 1/8 + 2/8$; $2\ 1/8 = 1 + 1 + 1/8 = 8/8 + 8/8 + 1/8$. c. Add and subtract mixed numbers with like denominators, e.g., by replacing each mixed number with an equivalent fraction, and/or by using properties of operations and the relationship between addition and subtraction. d. Solve word problems involving addition and subtraction of fractions referring to the same whole and having like denominators, e.g., by using visual fraction models and equations to represent the problem.	11, 105, 108, 123, 153, 155, 413, 525
4.NF.4	Apply and extend previous understandings of multiplication to multiply a fraction by a whole number. a. Understand a fraction a/b as a multiple of $1/b$. *For example, use a visual fraction model to represent* $5/4$ *as the product* $5 \times (1/4)$, *recording the conclusion by the equation* $5/4 = 5 \times (1/4)$. b. Understand a multiple of a/b as a multiple of $1/b$, and use this understanding to multiply a fraction by a whole number. *For example, use a visual fraction model to express* $3 \times (2/5)$ *as* $6 \times (1/5)$, *recognizing this product as* $6/5$. *(In general,* $n \times (a/b) = (n \times a)/b$.*)* c. Solve word problems involving multiplication of a fraction by a whole number, e.g., by using visual fraction models and equations to represent the problem. *For example, if each person at a party will eat 3/8 of a pound of roast beef, and there will be 5 people at the party, how many pounds of roast beef will be needed? Between what two whole numbers does your answer lie?*	108, 119, 188A, 528A
Understand decimal notation for fractions, and compare decimal fractions.		
4.NF.6	Use decimal notation for fractions with denominators 10 or 100. *For example, rewrite 0.62 as 62/100; describe a length as 0.62 meters; locate 0.62 on a number line diagram.*	11, 123, 153
4.NF.7	Compare two decimals to hundredths by reasoning about their size. Recognize that comparisons are valid only when the two decimals refer to the same whole. Record the results of comparisons with the symbols >, =, or <, and justify the conclusions, e.g., by using a visual model.	464

Grade 4 Standard Code	Descriptor	Teacher Edition Page Citations
Measurement and Data		
Solve problems involving measurement and conversion of measurements from a larger unit to a smaller unit.		
4.MD.1	Know relative sizes of measurement units within one system of units including km, m, cm; kg, g; lb, oz.; l, ml; hr, min, sec. Within a single system of measurement, express measurements in a larger unit in terms of a smaller unit. Record measurement equivalents in a two-column table. *For example, know that 1 ft is 12 times as long as 1 in. Express the length of a 4 ft snake as 48 in. Generate a conversion table for feet and inches listing the number pairs (1, 12), (2, 24), (3, 36), ...*	33, 76A, 83, 132A, 160, 162, 199, 249, 259A, 281, 287A, 288, 284A, 298, 307, 542
4.MD.2	Use the four operations to solve word problems involving distances, intervals of time, liquid volumes, masses of objects, and money, including problems involving simple fractions or decimals, and problems that require expressing measurements given in a larger unit in terms of a smaller unit. Represent measurement quantities using diagrams such as number line diagrams that feature a measurement scale.	87, 164A, 227, 357
4.MD.3	Apply the area and perimeter formulas for rectangles in real world and mathematical problems. *For example, find the width of a rectangular room given the area of the flooring and the length, by viewing the area formula as a multiplication equation with an unknown factor.*	40A
Represent and interpret data.		
4.MD.4	Make a line plot to display a data set of measurements in fractions of a unit (1/2, 1/4, 1/8). Solve problems involving addition and subtraction of fractions by using information presented in line plots. *For example, from a line plot find and interpret the difference in length between the longest and shortest specimens in an insect collection.*	132A, 288A, 394

Correlation to

ScienceSaurus

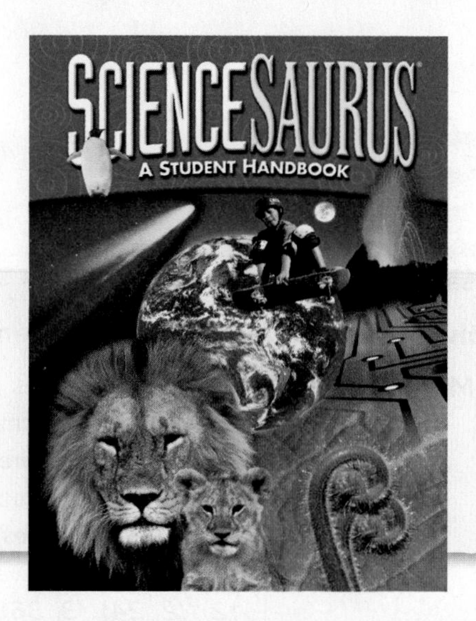

ScienceSaurus, ***A Student Handbook,*** is a "mini-encyclopedia" students can use to find out more about unit topics. It contains numerous resources including concise content summaries, an almanac, many tables, charts, and graphs, history of science, and a glossary. ***ScienceSaurus*** is available from Houghton Mifflin Harcourt..

ScienceFusion Grade 4	*ScienceSaurus* Topics	*ScienceSaurus* Pages
Unit 1 Studying Science		
Lesson 1 What Do Scientists Do?	Doing Science, Scientific Investigation Doing Science, Working Safely	pp. 2–27 pp. 28–37
Lesson 2 What Skills Do Scientists Use?	Doing Science, Scientific Investigation Doing Science, Using Science Tools and Equipment Doing Science, Using Tables and Graphs Almanac, Numbers in Science Almanac, Solving Math Problems in Science	pp. 2–27 pp. 38–59 pp. 60–73 pp. 371–379 pp. 380–385
Lesson 3 How Do Scientists Collect and Use Data?	Doing Science, Scientific Investigation Doing Science, Using Science Tools and Equipment Doing Science, Using Tables and Graphs Almanac, Maps	pp. 2–27 pp. 38–59 pp. 60–73 pp. 403–407
Lesson 4 Why Do Scientists Compare Results?	Doing Science, Scientific Investigation Doing Science, Using Science Tools and Equipment Doing Science, Using Tables and Graphs Almanac, Numbers in Science	pp. 2–27 pp. 38–59 pp. 60–73 pp. 371–379
People in Science—John Diebold/ Martin Culpepper	Science, Technology, and Society, Science and Society Yellow Pages, History of Science Yellow Pages, Science Time Line Yellow Pages, Famous Scientists and Inventors	pp. 364–369 p. 412 pp. 413–423 pp. 424–435
Lesson 5 What Kinds of Models Do Scientists Use?	Doing Science, Scientific Investigation Earth Science, Weather and Climate	pp. 2–27 pp. 198–217
Lesson 6 How Can You Model a School?	Doing Science, Scientific Investigation	pp. 2–27

ScienceFusion Grade 4	*ScienceSaurus* Topics	*ScienceSaurus* Pages
Unit 2 The Engineering Process		
Lesson 1 What Is an Engineering Design Process?	Science, Technology, and Society, Science and Technology	pp. 356–363
Lesson 2 How Can You Design a Solution to a Problem?	Science, Technology, and Society, Science and Technology	pp. 356–363
Lesson 3 What Is Technology?	Science, Technology, and Society, Science and Technology Science, Technology, and Society, Science and Society	pp. 356–363 pp. 364–369
Lesson 4 How Do We Use Technology?	Science, Technology, and Society, Science and Technology Science, Technology, and Society, Science and Society	pp. 356–363 pp. 364–369
People in Science—Ayanna Howard	Science, Technology, and Society, Science and Technology Science, Technology, and Society, Science and Society Yellow Pages, History of Science Yellow Pages, Science Time Line Yellow Pages, Famous Scientists and Inventors	pp. 356–363 pp. 364–369 p. 412 pp. 413–423 pp. 424–435

ScienceFusion Grade 4	*ScienceSaurus* Topics	*ScienceSaurus* Pages
Unit 3 Plants and Animals		
Lesson 1 What Are Some Plant Structures?	Life Science, Characteristics of Living Things Life Science, Cells, Tissues, Organs, and Systems	pp. 76–91 pp. 98–109
S.T.E.M. Engineering and Technology—Water Irrigation System	Science, Technology, and Society, Science and Technology Science, Technology, and Society, Science and Society	pp. 356–363 pp. 364–369
Lesson 2 How Do Plants Reproduce?	Life Science, Characteristics of Living Things	pp. 76–91
Lesson 3 How Can We Observe a Plant's Life Cycle?	Life Science, Characteristics of Living Things	pp. 76–91
Lesson 4 How Do Animals Reproduce?	Life Science, Characteristics of Living Things	pp. 76–91
Careers in Science—Animal Behaviorist	Life Science, Animal and Plant Behavior Science, Technology, and Society, Science and Technology Science, Technology, and Society, Science and Society	pp. 92–97 pp. 356–363 pp. 364–369
Lesson 5 How Are Living Things Adapted to Their Environment?	Life Science, Characteristics of Living Things Life Science, Animal and Plant Behavior Life Science, Ecology Life Science, Classifying Organisms	pp. 76–91 pp. 92–97 pp. 126–138 pp. 139–155
Lesson 6 Why Do Bird Beaks Differ?	Life Science, Characteristics of Living Things Life Science, Animal and Plant Behavior Life Science, Ecology Life Science, Classifying Organisms	pp. 76–91 pp. 92–97 pp. 126–138 pp. 139–155

ScienceFusion Grade 4	*ScienceSaurus* Topics	*ScienceSaurus* Pages
Unit 4 Energy and Ecosystems		
Lesson 1 What Are Populations, Habitats, and Niches?	Life Science, Ecology Natural Resources and the Environment, Conserving Resources	pp. 126–138 pp. 344–353
Lesson 2 What Are Food Chains?	Life Science, Ecology Natural Resources and the Environment, Conserving Resources	pp. 126–138 pp. 344–353
Lesson 3 How Can We Model a Food Web?	Life Science, Ecology Natural Resources and the Environment, Conserving Resources	pp. 126–138 pp. 344–353
Lesson 4 What Are Natural Resources?	Earth Science, Earth's Structure Natural Resources and the Environment, Natural Resources	pp. 158–169 pp. 320–333
Lesson 5 How Do People Impact Ecosystems?	Life Science, Ecology Natural Resources and the Environment, Pollution Natural Resources and the Environment, Conserving Resources	pp. 126–138 pp. 334–343 pp. 344–353
Lesson 6 How Do People Affect Their Environment?	Life Science, Ecology Natural Resources and the Environment, Pollution Natural Resources and the Environment, Protecting Resources	pp. 126–138 pp. 334–343 pp. 344–353
People in Science— Wangari Maathi/Willie Smits	Science, Technology, and Society, Science and Society Yellow Pages, History of Science Yellow Pages, Science Time Line Yellow Pages, Famous Scientists and Inventors	pp. 364–369 p. 412 pp. 413–423 pp. 424–435
S.T.E.M. Engineering and Technology—Underwater Exploration	Life Science, Ecology Science, Technology, and Society, Science and Technology Science, Technology, and Society, Science and Society	pp. 126–138 pp. 356–363 pp. 364–369

ScienceFusion Grade 4	*ScienceSaurus* Topics	*ScienceSaurus* Pages
Unit 5 Weather		
Lesson 1 What Is the Water Cycle?	Earth Science, Earth's Structure Earth Science, Water on Earth	pp. 158–170 pp. 187–197
Lesson 2 What Are Types of Weather?	Earth Science, Weather and Climate	pp. 198–217
Lesson 3 How Is Weather Predicted?	Earth Science, Weather and Climate	pp. 198–217
S.T.E.M. Engineering and Technology—Beaufort Wind Scale	Earth Science, Weather and Climate Science, Technology, and Society, Science and Technology Science, Technology, and Society, Science and Society	pp. 198–217 pp. 356–363 pp. 364–369
Lesson 4 How Can We Observe Weather Patterns?	Earth Science, Weather and Climate	pp. 198–217
People in Science—N. Christina Hsu	Science, Technology, and Society, Science and Society Yellow Pages, History of Science Yellow Pages, Science Time Line Yellow Pages, Famous Scientists and Inventors	pp. 364–369 p. 412 pp. 413–423 pp. 424–435
Unit 6 Earth and Space		
Lesson 1 How Do the Sun, Earth, and Moon Interact?	Earth Science, Earth and Its Moon Earth Science, The Solar System and Beyond	pp. 218–225 pp. 226–239
People in Science— Milutin Milankovitch/Maureen Raymo	Science, Technology, and Society, Science and Society Yellow Pages, History of Science Yellow Pages, Science Time Line Yellow Pages, Famous Scientists and Inventors	pp. 364–369 p. 412 pp. 413–423 pp. 424–435
Lesson 2 What Are Moon Phases?	Earth Science, Earth and Its Moon	pp. 218–225
Lesson 3 How Does the Moon Move Around Earth?	Earth Science, Earth and Its Moon	pp. 218–225
Lesson 4 What Are the Planets in Our Solar System?	Earth Science, The Solar System and Beyond	pp. 226–239
S.T.E.M. Engineering and Technology—Space Exploration	Science, Technology, and Society, Science and Technology Science, Technology, and Society, Science and Society	pp. 356–363 pp. 364–369
Lesson 5 How Can We Model the Sun and Planets?	Earth Science, The Solar System and Beyond	pp. 226–239

ScienceFusion Grade 4	*ScienceSaurus* Topics	*ScienceSaurus* Pages
Unit 7 Properties of Matter		
Lesson 1 What Are Physical Properties of Matter?	Physical Science, Matter	pp. 242–259
Lesson 2 How Are Physical Properties Observed?	Physical Science, Matter	pp. 242–259
Careers in Science—Materials Scientists	Science, Technology, and Society, Science and Technology Science, Technology, and Society, Science and Society	pp. 356–363 pp. 364–369
Lesson 3 What Is Conservation of Mass?	Physical Science, Matter Physical Science, Changes in Matter	pp. 242–259 pp. 260–267
Lesson 4 What Are the States of Water?	Physical Science, Changes in Matter	pp. 260–267
S.T.E.M. Engineering and Technology—Refrigeration	Science, Technology, and Society, Science and Technology Science, Technology, and Society, Science and Society	pp. 356–363 pp. 364–369
Unit 8 Changes in Matter		
Lesson 1 What Are Some Physical Changes?	Physical Science, Changes in Matter	pp. 260–267
Lesson 2 How Can We Make a Solution?	Physical Science, Matter Physical Science, Changes in Matter	pp. 242–259 pp. 260–267
Lesson 3 What Are Some Chemical Changes?	Physical Science, Changes in Matter	pp. 260–267
S.T.E.M. Engineering and Technology—Body Armor	Science, Technology, and Society, Science and Technology Science, Technology, and Society, Science and Society	pp. 356–363 pp. 364–369
Lesson 4 How Can You Tell When a New Substance Forms?	Physical Science, Changes in Matter	pp. 260–267
People in Science—Ruth Rogan Benerito/Hèctor Abruña	Science, Technology, and Society, Science and Society Yellow Pages, History of Science Yellow Pages, Science Time Line Yellow Pages, Famous Scientists and Inventors	pp. 364–369 p. 412 pp. 413–423 pp. 424–435

ScienceFusion Grade 4	*ScienceSaurus* Topics	*ScienceSaurus* Pages
Unit 9 Energy		
Lesson 1 What Are Some Forms of Energy?	Physical Science, Energy Physical Science, Heat Physical Science Electricity and Magnetism Physical Science, Light and Sound	pp. 284–287 pp. 288–294 pp. 295–307 pp. 308–317
Lesson 2 Where Does Energy Come From?	Physical Science, Energy	pp. 284–287
Lesson 3 What Is Heat?	Physical Science, Heat	pp. 288–294
Lesson 4 How Is Heat Produced?	Physical Science, Heat	pp. 288–294
Careers in Science— Geothermal Technician	Physical Science, Heat Science, Technology, and Society, Science and Technology Science, Technology, and Society, Science and Society	pp. 288–294 pp. 356–363 pp. 364–369
Lesson 5 What Are Conductors and Insulators?	Physical Science, Heat	pp. 288–294
Lesson 6 Which Materials Are Conductors?	Physical Science, Heat	pp. 288–294
S.T.E.M. Engineering and Technology—Piezoelectricity	Science, Technology, and Society, Science and Technology Science, Technology, and Society, Science and Society	pp. 356–363 pp. 364–369
Unit 10 Electricity		
Lesson 1 What Is Electricity?	Physical Science, Electricity and Magnetism	pp. 295–307
Lesson 2 How Do Electric Charges Interact?	Physical Science, Electricity and Magnetism	pp. 295–307
Lesson 3 What Is an Electric Circuit?	Physical Science, Electricity and Magnetism	pp. 295–307
Lesson 4 What Are Electric Circuits, Conductors, and Insulators?	Physical Science, Electricity and Magnetism	pp. 295–307
Careers in Science—Electrician	Physical Science, Electricity and Magnetism Science, Technology, and Society, Science and Technology Science, Technology, and Society, Science and Society	pp. 295–307 pp. 356–363 pp. 364–369
Lesson 5 How Do We Use Electricity?	Physical Science, Electricity and Magnetism	pp. 295–307

ScienceFusion Grade 4	*ScienceSaurus* Topics	*ScienceSaurus* Pages
Unit 10 Electricity (continued)		
S.T.E.M. Engineering and Technology—The Electric Grid	Science, Technology, and Society, Science and Technology Science, Technology, and Society, Science and Society	pp. 356–363 pp. 364–369
Unit 11 Motion		
Lesson 1 What Is Motion?	Physical Science, Forces and Motion	pp. 268–283
Lesson 2 What Is Speed?	Physical Science, Forces and Motion	pp. 268–283
Careers in Science—Air Traffic Controller	Science, Technology, and Society, Science and Technology Science, Technology, and Society, Science and Society	pp. 356–363 pp. 364–369
S.T.E.M. Engineering and Technology—Gyroscopes	Science, Technology, and Society, Science and Technology Science, Technology, and Society, Science and Society	pp. 356–363 pp. 364–369
All Units		
These topics may be used with all units and lessons.	Almanac, Numbers in Science Almanac, Solving Math Problems in Science Almanac, Study Skills Almanac, Test-Taking Skills Almanac, Maps Almanac, Measurement Tables Yellow Pages, Science Word Parts Yellow Pages, Glossary of Science Terms	pp. 371–379 pp. 380–385 pp. 386–393 pp. 394–402 pp. 403–407 pp. 408–410 pp. 436–437 pp. 438–493
These topics may be used with all investigations.	Doing Science, Scientific Investigation Doing Science, Working Safely Doing Science, Using Science Tools and Equipment Doing Science, Using Tables and Graphs	pp. 2–27 pp. 28–37 pp. 38–59 pp. 60–73
These topics may be used with all S.T.E.M. features and S.T.E.M. investigations.	Science, Technology, and Society, Science and Technology Science, Technology, and Society, Science and Society	pp. 356–363 pp. 364–369
These topics are covered at another grade.	Human Body Systems Earth Science, Earth's Changing Surface	pp. 110–125 pp. 170–186

Grade-Level Materials Lists

Quantities are indicated for one group of students.

Guided Inquiry and S.T.E.M. Lessons

The following list provides materials needed for all the Guided Inquiry and STEM Lessons—the core activities—in this grade level.

Nonconsumable Materials

Material	Quantity per Group	Teacher Edition Page
apron, lab	varies	403A
balance	1	41A, 367A, 371A
ball, foam	1	325A, 445A
ball, tennis	1	367A
battery holder	1	499A
beaker, 250 mL	1	403A
bin, plastic, large	1	233A
books	varies	93A, 367A
bowl, plastic, small	varies	165A
chair	1	325A
classroom objects	varies	41A, 367A, 371A
comb, plastic	1	476A
compass	1	342A
compass, drawing	1	343A
computer	1	55A
container, plastic, clear 16 oz	1	558A
dowel, wooden	1	459A
dropper	1	165A, 418A
flashlight	1	325A
forceps	1	133A, 165A, 419A
graduated cylinder, 100 mL	1	165A
hand lens	1	419A
jar, plastic, clear, 16 oz	1	476A
key	1	367A

Nonconsumable Materials (continued)

Material	Quantity per Group	Teacher Edition Page
knife, metal, butter	1	473A
lid, metal	1	93A
light bulb holder	1	459A
light socket, mini	varies	499A
light socket, porcelain	varies	459A
marble	varies	93A, 558A
media resources	varies	116A, 238A, 286A, 342A, 384A, 418A, 476A, 530A, 558A
nails, finishing	varies	530A
needle	1	459A
petri dish	1	419A
pictures, bird	varies	165A
pushpin	varies	343A
safety goggles	varies	403A, 418A, 419A, 459A
scissors	1	205A, 342A, 343A, 459A
spoon, slotted	1	165A
spring scale, 5 kg/50 N	1	41A, 93A, 384A
stopwatch	1	473A, 553A
switch with clips	1	499A, 530A
tape measure	1	41A, 55A, 553A
thermometer	1	476A
tubing	varies	558A
weather check tool	1	287A
weather station	1	287A

Nonconsumable Materials (continued)

Material	Quantity per Group	Teacher Edition Page
wire cutter, stripper	1	165A
wood, blocks	varies	93A

Consumable Materials

Material	Quantity per Group	Teacher Edition Page
alcohol	1	403A
apple core	1	233A
bag, freezer, 1 gal	1	77A
baking soda	varies	418A
banana peel	1	233A
battery, size D	varies	325A, 499A, 530A
box, cardboard	1	55A, 77A
butter	varies	473A
can, soda	1	233A
cardboard	varies	558A
classroom art supplies	varies	286A
clay, modeling	varies	205A, 342A, 384A
cotton balls	varies	77A
cup, clear plastic, 16 oz	1	233A, 403A, 473A
cup, plastic, 9 oz	1	133A
egg	1	77A
fabric	varies	77A
fiber fill	varies	77A
foil, aluminum	varies	476A
gloves, disposable	1	233A, 403A
glue stick	1	205A
grapes	varies	165A
graphite, pencil lead	varies	499A
gummy worms	varies	165A

Consumable Materials (continued)

Material	Quantity per Group	Teacher Edition Page
index cards	varies	205A, 384A
juice	1	165A
knife, plastic	1	473A
lettuce	1	165A
light bulb, miniature	1	499A
magazines	varies	205A
markers	1	133A, 205A, 342A, 343A, 384A, 473A
newspaper	varies	233A
paint, black	varies	476A
paper	varies	116A, 238A, 286A, 325A, 342A, 384A, 459A
paper, butcher block	varies	343A
paper, construction	varies	205A, 343A
paper, drawing	varies	55A
paper, graph	varies	55A
paper, towel	varies	133A, 403A
paper clips	varies	367A, 384A, 499A, 530A
peanuts, foam	varies	77A
pencil	1	116A, 238A, 286A, 325A, 342A, 343A, 367A, 384A, 459A
plastic wrap	varies	133A, 476A
plate, plastic	varies	418A
rice	varies	165A
rubber band	1	384A

Consumable Materials (continued)

Material	Quantity per Group	Teacher Edition Page
sand, fine	varies	165A
seeds, lima bean	1	133A
seeds, pumpkin	1	133A
seeds, sunflower	varies	133A, 165A
shoebox	1	205A, 476A
soil, potting	varies	233A
spoon, plastic	1	233A, 403A, 418A
steel wool	varies	419A
sticks, craft	varies	499A
straw, plastic, drinking	varies	165A
string, cotton	varies	93A, 205A, 343A
sugar	varies	403A
tape, masking	varies	133A, 325A, 384A, 553A, 558A
thread	varies	459A
toothpicks	varies	205A
vinegar	1	418A
wire, insulated	varies	499A, 530A
yarn	varies	77A

Directed and Independent Activities

The following list provides materials needed for the optional Directed and Independent activities in this grade level. The * indicates materials that also appear on the Guided Inquiry materials list.

Nonconsumable Materials

Material	Quantity per Group	Teacher Edition Page
apron, lab *	varies	391A, 403A, 447A
balance *	1	41A, 351A, 367A, 371A
ball, foam *	1	325A, 445A
ball, tennis *	1	367A, 553A
basketball	1	297A
battery holder *	1	499A, 501A
beaker, 250 mL *	1	221A, 245A, 351A, 373A, 403A
bin, plastic, large *	1	233A
blender	1	207A
board, flat	1	207A
books *	varies	93A, 367A
bottle, spray trigger	1	173A
bowl, plastic, large	1	151A
bowl, plastic, small	varies	165A
box, plastic	1	259A
bulb, compact *	varies	459A
chair *	1	325A
classroom objects *	varies	41A, 63A, 351A, 367A, 371A
cloth, silk	1	497A
cloth, wool	1	483A, 497A
clothespin *	varies	165A
comb, plastic *	1	476A, 483A
compass *	1	342A, 517A
compass, drawing *	1	343A

Nonconsumable Materials (continued)

Material	Quantity per Group	Teacher Edition Page
computer *	1	55A
container, plastic, clear 16 oz *	1	27A, 558A
dominoes	varies	79A
dowel, wooden *	1	445A, 459A
dropper *	1	165A, 391A, 418A
fan	1	245A
flashlight	1	297A, 325A
forceps *	1	133A, 165A, 419A
fur, fake	1	151A, 483A
graduated cylinder, 100 mL *	1	165A, 351A
hand lens *	1	117A, 135A, 419A
jar, plastic, clear, 16 oz *	1	135A, 447A, 476A, 483A
key	1	367A
knife, metal, butter	1	473A
lid, metal *	1	93A, 135A
light bulb holder *	1	459A
hook	varies	79A
hot plate	1	373A
lamp	1	135A, 447A, 517A
light socket, mini	varies	499A, 501A
light socket, porcelain *	varies	459A
marble *	varies	79A, 93A, 558A
media resources *	varies	27A, 63A, 116A, 117A, 151A, 173A, 189A, 238A, 273A, 286A, 297A, 315A, 327A, 342A, 384A, 418A, 429A, 463A, 476A, 530A, 558A
mesh screen	1	207A

Directed and Independent Activities (continued)

Nonconsumable Materials (continued)

Material	Quantity per Group	Teacher Edition Page
mitts, oven	1	373A
nails, finishing *	varies	517A, 530A
needle *	1	459A
pan, aluminum, 13" x 9" x 2"	1	245A, 259A
pennies	varies	45A
petri dish *	1	419A
pictures, bird *	varies	165A
pitcher	1	273A
pushpin *	varies	327A, 343A
refrigerator	1	135A
ruler	1	17A, 27A, 45A, 463A
safety goggles *	varies	3A, 173A, 373A, 391A, 403A, 405A, 418A, 419A, 445A, 447A, 459A
scissors *	1	3A, 17A, 45A, 189A, 205A, 342A, 343A, 459A, 463A
spoon, measuring 4-in-1	1	221A
spoon, slotted *	1	165A
spring	1	445A
spring scale, 5 kg/50 N *	1	41A, 93A, 384A
stopwatch *	1	17A, 151A, 273A, 473A, 537A, 553A

Nonconsumable Materials (continued)

Material	Quantity per Group	Teacher Edition Page
switch with clips *	1	499A, 501A, 530A
table	2	45A
tape measure *	1	3A, 17A, 27A, 41A, 45A, 55A, 79A, 103A, 221A, 327A, 445A, 537A, 553A
thermometer *	1	151A, 259A, 447A, 463A, 476A
tubing *	varies	558A
washer, metal, 1 ½"	varies	17A
washer, metal, ¾"	varies	17A
weather check tool *	1	287A
weather station *	1	287A
wire cutter, stripper *	1	165A
wood, blocks *	varies	93A

Consumable Materials

Material	Quantity per Group	Teacher Edition Page
alcohol *	1	351A, 391A, 403A
antacid tablets	varies	405A
apple core *	1	233A
bag, freezer, 1 gal *	1	77A, 151A
baking powder	varies	17A
baking soda	varies	17A, 405A, 418A
ball, foam	1	445A
balloon, round	1	497A
banana peel *	1	233A
battery, size D *	varies	297A, 325A, 499A, 501A, 517A, 530A
bottle, clear, plastic, 16 oz	1	447A
bottle, clear, plastic, 2 L	2	173A
box, cardboard *	1	55A, 77A
brine shrimp	1	135A
butter *	varies	473A
calendar, blank	1	315A
candy	1	79A
can, soda *	1	233A
cardboard *	varies	327A, 558A
cardboard, strip	varies	79A
celery, leafy	1	103A
cereal, puffed rice	1	483A
classroom art supplies *	varies	207A, 221A, 286A, 429A
clay, modeling *	varies	27A, 205A, 342A, 384A, 447A

Consumable Materials (continued)

Material	Quantity per Group	Teacher Edition Page
corn syrup	1	391A
cotton balls *	varies	77A
cup, clear plastic, 16 oz *	1	103A, 233A, 259A, 273A, 403A, 473A
cup, paper, 12 oz	1	45A
cup, plastic, 9 oz *	1	133A, 405A
detergent	1	391A
dryer sheet	1	483A
egg *	1	77A
eggshells	varies	405A
fabric *	varies	77A
fiber fill *	varies	77A
flower	1	117A
foil, aluminum	varies	463A, 476A
food coloring	1	103A, 447A
gloves, disposable *	1	151A, 173A, 233A, 403A
glue	1	189A, 463A
glue stick *	1	205A
glycerin	1	391A
grapes *	varies	165A
graphite, pencil lead *	varies	499A
gummy worms *	varies	165A
ice cubes	varies	151A, 245A, 273A, 373A
index cards *	varies	3A, 205A, 245A, 259A, 384A, 537A
index cards, blue	varies	429A

Directed and Independent Activities (continued)

Consumable Materials (continued)

Material	Quantity per Group	Teacher Edition Page
index cards, yellow	varies	429A
juice *	1	165A
knife, plastic	1	473A
lettuce *	1	165A
light bulb, incandescent	1	459A
light bulb, fluorescent	1	459A
light bulb, miniature *	1	499A, 501A
magazines *	varies	189A, 205A
markers *	set	27A, 63A, 133A, 189A, 205A, 207A, 221A, 245A, 297A, 342A, 343A, 384A, 473A
molasses	1	351A
newspaper *	varies	207A, 233A
oil, vegetable	1	351A, 391A
paint, black *	varies	476A
paper *	varies	3A, 17A, 27A, 45A, 63A, 79A, 103A, 116A, 117A, 173A, 189A, 238A, 245A, 286A, 297A, 325A, 327A, 342A, 351A, 384A, 391A, 429A, 459A, 463A, 483A
paper, butcher block	varies	343A
paper, construction *	varies	189A, 205A, 343A, 447A
paper, drawing *	varies	55A
paper, graph *	varies	55A

Consumable Materials (continued)

Material	Quantity per Group	Teacher Edition Page
paper, towel *	varies	103A, 133A, 403A
paper clips *	varies	3A, 45A, 367A, 384A, 499A, 517A, 530A
peanuts, foam *	varies	77A
pebbles	varies	173A
pencil *	1	3A, 17A, 27A, 45A, 63A, 79A, 103A, 116A, 117A, 173A, 189A, 238A, 245A, 259A, 286A, 297A, 325A, 327A, 342A, 343A, 351A, 367A, 384A, 391A, 429A, 459A, 463A, 483A
pencil, colored	varies	117A, 173A, 327A
pen	1	429A
plants	2	103A, 173A, 221A
plastic wrap *	varies	133A, 173A, 476A, 483A
plate, plastic *	varies	391A, 418A, 483A
poster board	1	463A
rice *	varies	165A
rubber band *	1	173A, 384A
salt	varies	373A
sand, coarse	varies	173A
sand, fine *	varies	165A, 259A
seeds, lima bean *	1	133A
seeds, pumpkin *	1	133A
seeds, sunflower *	varies	133A, 165A
shoebox *	1	79A, 205A, 476A

Consumable Materials (continued)

Material	Quantity per Group	Teacher Edition Page
shoebox lid	1	463A
shortening	1	151A
soil, potting *	varies	173A, 233A
spoon, plastic *	1	173A, 233A, 403A, 405A, 418A
steel wool	varies	419A
straw, plastic, drinking *	varies	45A, 165A, 447A
sticks, craft *	varies	499A
string, cotton *	varies	17A, 79A, 93A, 189A, 205A, 327A, 343A, 463A, 497A
sugar *	varies	17A, 403A
tape, masking *	varies	45A, 79A, 133A, 325A, 384A, 445A, 447A, 497A, 537A, 553A, 558A
tape, transparent	varies	517A
thread *	varies	459A
toothpicks *	varies	205A, 373A
vinegar *	1	17A, 221A, 405A, 418A
wax worm	varies	135A
wax worm, food	varies	135A
wire, insulated *	varies	517A, 499A, 501A, 530A
yarn *	varies	77A

For more information about Materials Kits, contact your Houghton Mifflin Harcourt sales representative.

Student Edition

Interactive Glossary

Interactive Glossary

As you learn about each term, add notes, drawings, or sentences in the extra space. This will help you remember what the terms mean. Here are some examples.

Fungi [FUHN•jeye] A kingdom of organisms that have a nucleus and get nutrients by decomposing other organisms

A mushroom is from the kingdom Fungi.

physical change [FIZ•ih•kuhl CHAYNJ] Change in the size, shape, or state of matter with no new substance being formed

When I cut paper, the paper has a physical change.

Glossary Pronunciation Key

With every glossary term, there is also a phonetic respelling. A phonetic respelling writes the word the way it sounds, which can help you pronounce new or unfamiliar words. Use this key to help you understand the respellings.

Sound	As in	Phonetic Respelling	Sound	As in	Phonetic Respelling
a	bat	(BAT)	oh	over	(OH•ver)
ah	lock	(LAHK)	oo	pool	(POOL)
air	rare	(RAIR)	ow	out	(OWT)
ar	argue	(AR•gyoo)	oy	foil	(FOYL)
aw	law	(LAW)	s	cell	(SEL)
ay	face	(FAYS)		sit	(SIT)
ch	chapel	(CHAP•uhl)	sh	sheep	(SHEEP)
e	test	(TEST)	th	that	(THAT)
	metric	(MEH•trik)		thin	(THIN)
ee	eat	(EET)	u	pull	(PUL)
	feet	(FEET)	uh	medal	(MED•uhl)
	ski	(SKEE)		talent	(TAL•uhnt)
er	paper	(PAY•per)		pencil	(PEN•suhl)
	fern	(FERN)		onion	(UHN•yuhn)
eye	idea	(eye•DEE•uh)		playful	(PLAY•fuhl)
i	bit	(BIT)		dull	(DUHL)
ing	going	(GOH•ing)	y	yes	(YES)
k	card	(KARD)		ripe	(RYP)
	kite	(KYT)	z	bags	(BAGZ)
ngk	bank	(BANGK)	zh	treasure	(TREZH•er)

R1

Interactive Glossary

A

acceleration [ak•sel•er•AY•shuhn] Any change in the speed or direction of an object's motion (p. 544)

adaptation [ad•uhp•TAY•shuhn] A trait or characteristic that helps an organism survive (p. 154)

air mass [AIR MAS] A large body of air that has the same temperature and humidity throughout (p. 276)

air pressure [AIR PRESH•er] The weight of the atmosphere pressing down on Earth (p. 261)

atmosphere [AT•muhs•feer] The mixture of gases that surround Earth (p. 247)

axis [AK•sis] The imaginary line around which Earth rotates (p. 298)

B

behavioral adaptation [bih•HAYV•yu•ruhl ad•uhp•TAY•shuhn] Something an animal does that helps it survive (p. 159)

R2

Interactive Glossary

C

carnivore [KAHR•nuh•vawr] An animal that eats only other animals (p. 192)

change of state [CHAYNJ uhv STAYT] A physical change that occurs when matter changes from one state to another, such as from a liquid to a gas (p. 378)

chemical change [KEM•ih•kuhl CHAYNJ] A change in one or more substances, caused by a reaction, that forms new and different substances (p. 408)

chemical energy [KEM•ih•kuhl EN•er•jee] Energy that can be released by a chemical reaction (p. 437)

chemical property [KEM•ih•kuhl PRAHP•er•tee] A property that involves how a substance interacts with other substances (p. 406)

chemical reaction [KEM•ih•kuhl ree•AK•shuhn] A chemical change (p. 411)

chlorophyll [KLAWR•uh•fihl] A green pigment in plants that allows plant cells to make food using sunlight (p. 110)

circuit [SER•kuht] A path along which electric charges can flow (p. 504)

R3

Interactive Glossary

community [kuh•MYOO•nih•tee] All of the organisms that live in the same place (p. 176)

complete metamorphosis [kuhm•PLEET met•uh•MAWR•fuh•sis] A complex change that most insects undergo that includes larva and pupa stages (p. 141)

computer model [kuhm•PYOO•ter MOD•l] A computer program that models an event or object (p. 49)

condensation [kahn•duhn•SAY•shuhn] The process by which a gas changes into a liquid (pp. 248, 379)

conduction [kuhn•DUK•shuhn] The movement of heat between two materials that are touching (p. 450)

conductor [kuhn•DUK•ter] A material that lets heat or electricity travel through it easily (pp. 464, 502)

conservation [kahn•ser•VAY•shuhn] The use of less of something to make its supply last longer (p. 228)

constellation [kahn•stuh•LAY•shuhn] A pattern of stars that form an imaginary picture or design in the sky (p. 304)

R4

Interactive Glossary

consumer [kuhn•SOOM•er] Animals that eat plants or other animals to get energy (p. 181)

convection [kuhn•VEK•shuhn] The transfer of heat within a liquid or a gas (p. 451)

D

data [DEY•tuh] Individual facts, statistics, and items of information (p. 35)

decomposer [dee•kuhm•POHZ•er] A living thing that gets energy by breaking down wastes and the remains of plants and animals (p. 181)

density [DEN•suh•tee] The amount of matter present in a certain volume of a substance (p. 358)

design [dih•ZYN] To conceive something and to prepare the plans and drawings for it to be built (p. 66)

E

ecosystem [EE•koh•sis•tuhm] A community of organisms and the physical environment in which they live (p. 174)

electric current [ee•LEK•trik KER•uhnt] The flow of electric charges along a path (p. 490)

R5

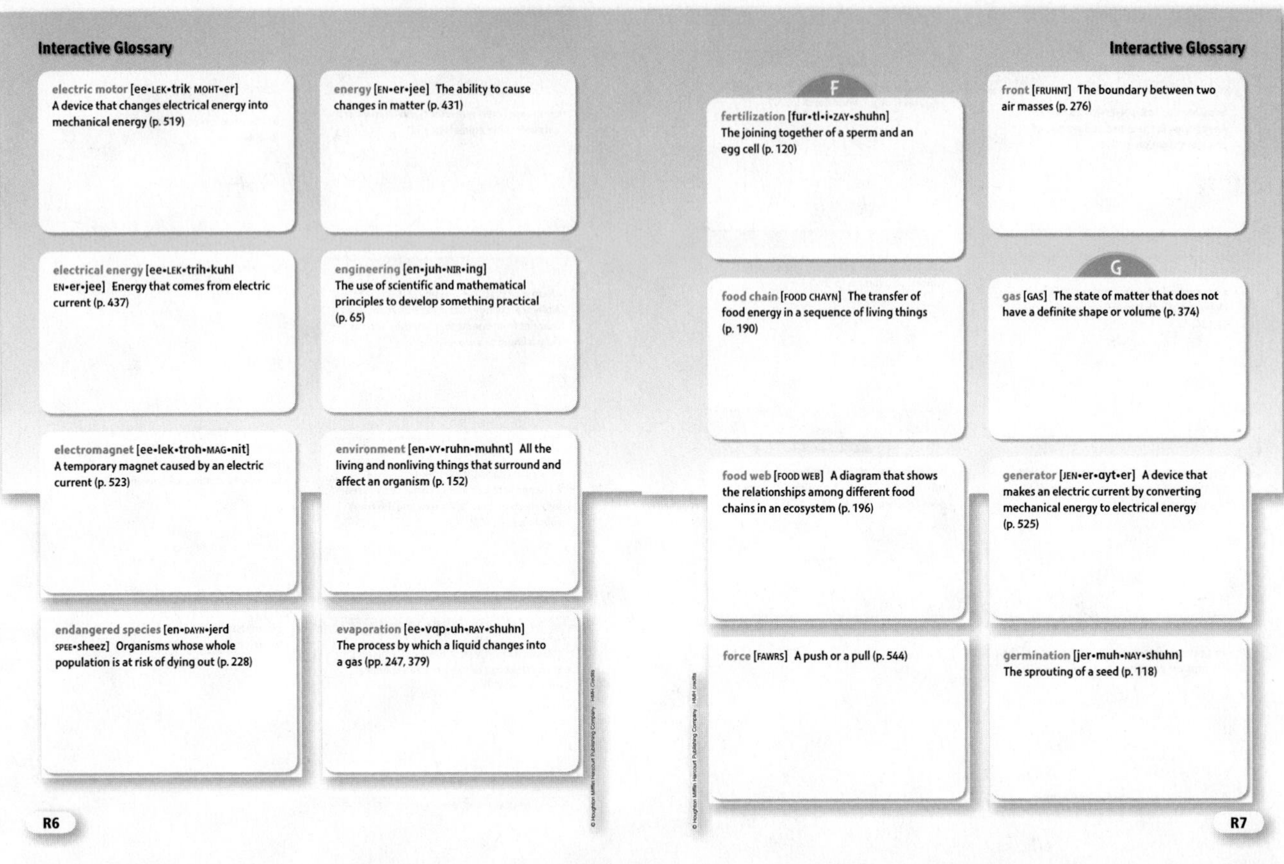

Interactive Glossary

electric motor [ee•LEK•trik MOHT•er] A device that changes electrical energy into mechanical energy (p. 519)

electrical energy [ee•LEK•trih•kuhl EN•er•jee] Energy that comes from electric current (p. 437)

electromagnet [ee•lek•troh•MAG•nit] A temporary magnet caused by an electric current (p. 523)

endangered species [en•DAYN•jerd SPEE•sheez] Organisms whose whole population is at risk of dying out (p. 228)

energy [EN•er•jee] The ability to cause changes in matter (p. 431)

engineering [en•juh•NIR•ing] The use of scientific and mathematical principles to develop something practical (p. 65)

environment [en•VY•ruhn•muhnt] All the living and nonliving things that surround and affect an organism (p. 152)

evaporation [ee•vap•uh•RAY•shuhn] The process by which a liquid changes into a gas (pp. 247, 379)

R6

Interactive Glossary

F

fertilization [fur•tl•i•ZAY•shuhn] The joining together of a sperm and an egg cell (p. 120)

food chain [FOOD CHAYN] The transfer of food energy in a sequence of living things (p. 190)

food web [FOOD WEB] A diagram that shows the relationships among different food chains in an ecosystem (p. 196)

force [FAWRS] A push or a pull (p. 544)

front [FRUHNT] The boundary between two air masses (p. 276)

G

gas [GAS] The state of matter that does not have a definite shape or volume (p. 374)

generator [JEN•er•ayt•er] A device that makes an electric current by converting mechanical energy to electrical energy (p. 525)

germination [jer•muh•NAY•shuhn] The sprouting of a seed (p. 118)

R7

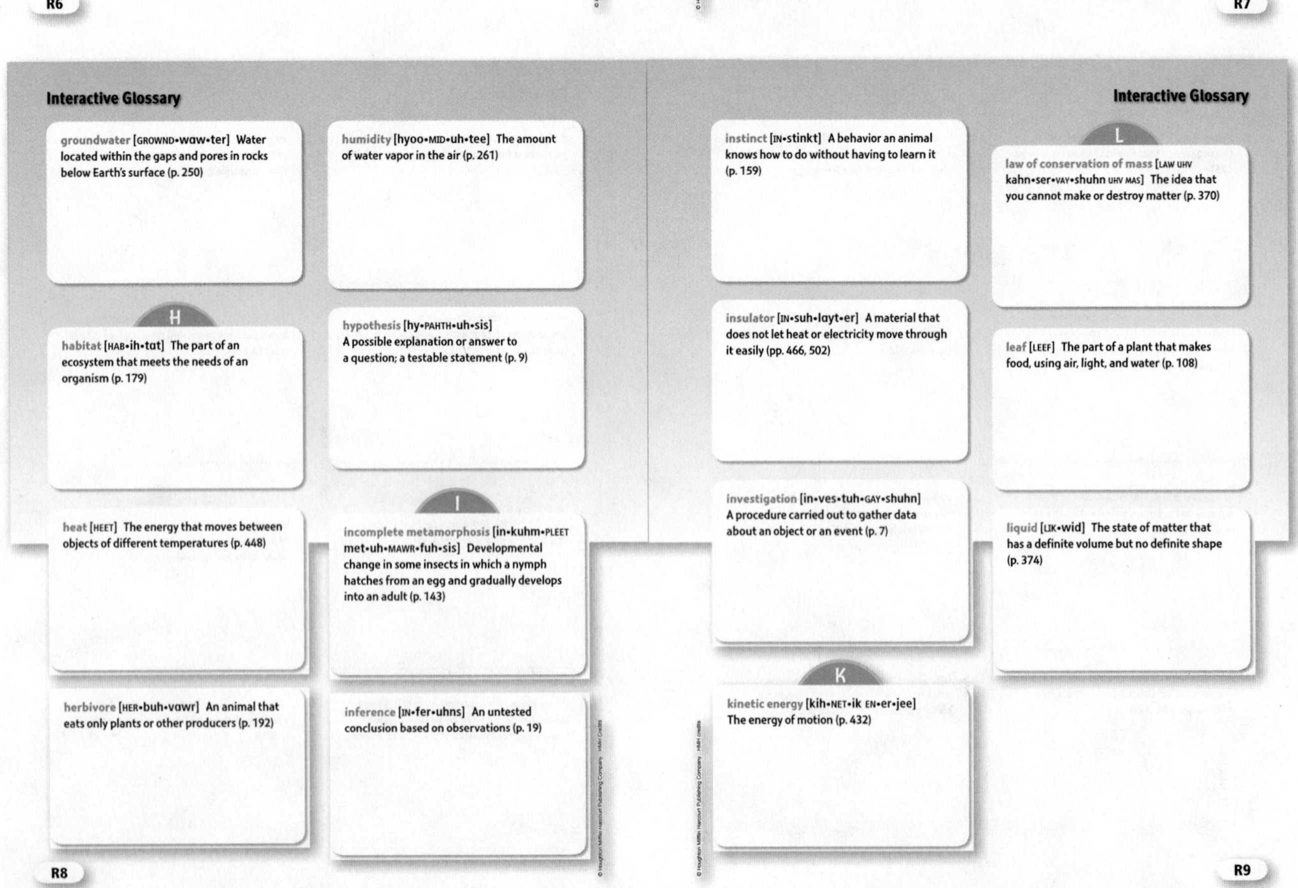

Interactive Glossary

groundwater [GROWND•waw•ter] Water located within the gaps and pores in rocks below Earth's surface (p. 250)

H

habitat [HAB•ih•tat] The part of an ecosystem that meets the needs of an organism (p. 179)

heat [HEET] The energy that moves between objects of different temperatures (p. 448)

herbivore [HER•buh•vawr] An animal that eats only plants or other producers (p. 192)

humidity [hyoo•MID•uh•tee] The amount of water vapor in the air (p. 261)

hypothesis [hy•PAHTH•uh•sis] A possible explanation or answer to a question; a testable statement (p. 9)

I

incomplete metamorphosis [in•kuhm•PLEET met•uh•MAWR•fuh•sis] Developmental change in some insects in which a nymph hatches from an egg and gradually develops into an adult (p. 143)

inference [IN•fer•uhns] An untested conclusion based on observations (p. 19)

R8

Interactive Glossary

instinct [IN•stinkt] A behavior an animal knows how to do without having to learn it (p. 159)

insulator [IN•suh•layt•er] A material that does not let heat or electricity move through it easily (pp. 466, 502)

investigation [in•ves•tuh•GAY•shuhn] A procedure carried out to gather data about an object or an event (p. 7)

K

kinetic energy [kih•NET•ik EN•er•jee] The energy of motion (p. 432)

L

law of conservation of mass [LAW UHV kahn•ser•VAY•shuhn UHV MAS] The idea that you cannot make or destroy matter (p. 370)

leaf [LEEF] The part of a plant that makes food, using air, light, and water (p. 108)

liquid [LIK•wid] The state of matter that has a definite volume but no definite shape (p. 374)

R9

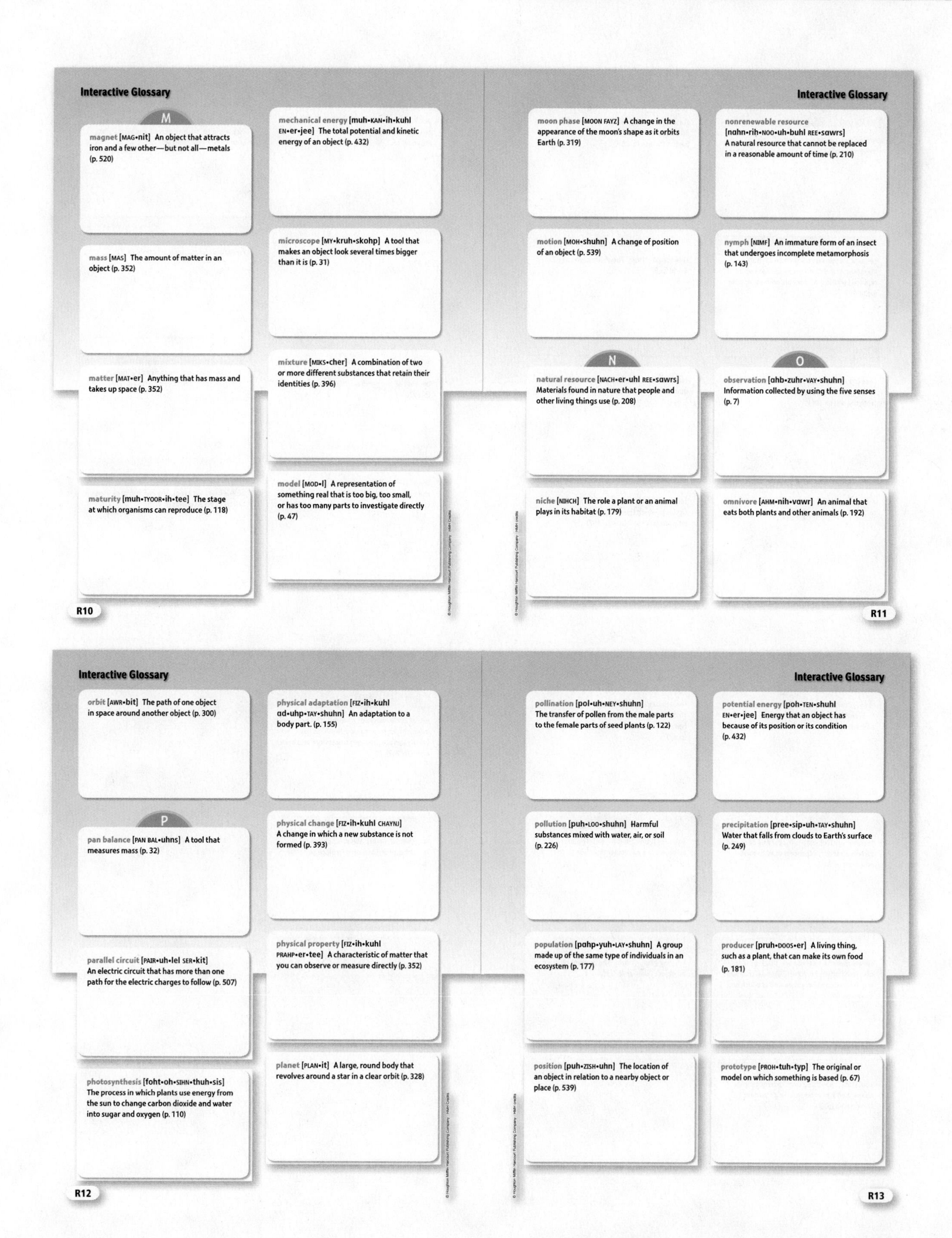

Interactive Glossary

M

magnet [MAG•nit] An object that attracts iron and a few other—but not all—metals (p. 520)

mass [MAS] The amount of matter in an object (p. 352)

matter [MAT•er] Anything that has mass and takes up space (p. 352)

maturity [muh•TYOOR•ih•tee] The stage at which organisms can reproduce (p. 118)

mechanical energy [muh•KAN•ih•kuhl EN•er•jee] The total potential and kinetic energy of an object (p. 432)

microscope [MY•kruh•skohp] A tool that makes an object look several times bigger than it is (p. 31)

mixture [MIKS•cher] A combination of two or more different substances that retain their identities (p. 396)

model [MOD•l] A representation of something real that is too big, too small, or has too many parts to investigate directly (p. 47)

R10

Interactive Glossary

moon phase [MOON FAYZ] A change in the appearance of the moon's shape as it orbits Earth (p. 319)

motion [MOH•shuhn] A change of position of an object (p. 539)

nonrenewable resource [nahn•rih•NOO•uh•buhl REE•sawrs] A natural resource that cannot be replaced in a reasonable amount of time (p. 210)

nymph [NIMF] An immature form of an insect that undergoes incomplete metamorphosis (p. 143)

N

natural resource [NACH•er•uhl REE•sawrs] Materials found in nature that people and other living things use (p. 208)

niche [NIHCH] The role a plant or an animal plays in its habitat (p. 179)

O

observation [ahb•zuhr•VAY•shuhn] Information collected by using the five senses (p. 7)

omnivore [AHM•nih•vawr] An animal that eats both plants and other animals (p. 192)

R11

Interactive Glossary

orbit [AWR•bit] The path of one object in space around another object (p. 300)

P

pan balance [PAN BAL•uhns] A tool that measures mass (p. 32)

parallel circuit [PAIR•uh•lel SER•kit] An electric circuit that has more than one path for the electric charges to follow (p. 507)

photosynthesis [foht•oh•SIHN•thuh•sis] The process in which plants use energy from the sun to change carbon dioxide and water into sugar and oxygen (p. 110)

physical adaptation [FIZ•ih•kuhl ad•uhp•TAY•shuhn] An adaptation to a body part. (p. 155)

physical change [FIZ•ih•kuhl CHAYNJ] A change in which a new substance is not formed (p. 393)

physical property [FIZ•ih•kuhl PRAHP•er•tee] A characteristic of matter that you can observe or measure directly (p. 352)

planet [PLAN•it] A large, round body that revolves around a star in a clear orbit (p. 328)

R12

Interactive Glossary

pollination [pol•uh•NEY•shuhn] The transfer of pollen from the male parts to the female parts of seed plants (p. 122)

pollution [puh•LOO•shuhn] Harmful substances mixed with water, air, or soil (p. 226)

population [pahp•yuh•LAY•shuhn] A group made up of the same type of individuals in an ecosystem (p. 177)

position [puh•ZISH•uhn] The location of an object in relation to a nearby object or place (p. 539)

potential energy [poh•TEN•shuhl EN•er•jee] Energy that an object has because of its position or its condition (p. 432)

precipitation [pree•sip•uh•TAY•shuhn] Water that falls from clouds to Earth's surface (p. 249)

producer [pruh•DOOS•er] A living thing, such as a plant, that can make its own food (p. 181)

prototype [PROH•tuh•typ] The original or model on which something is based (p. 67)

R13

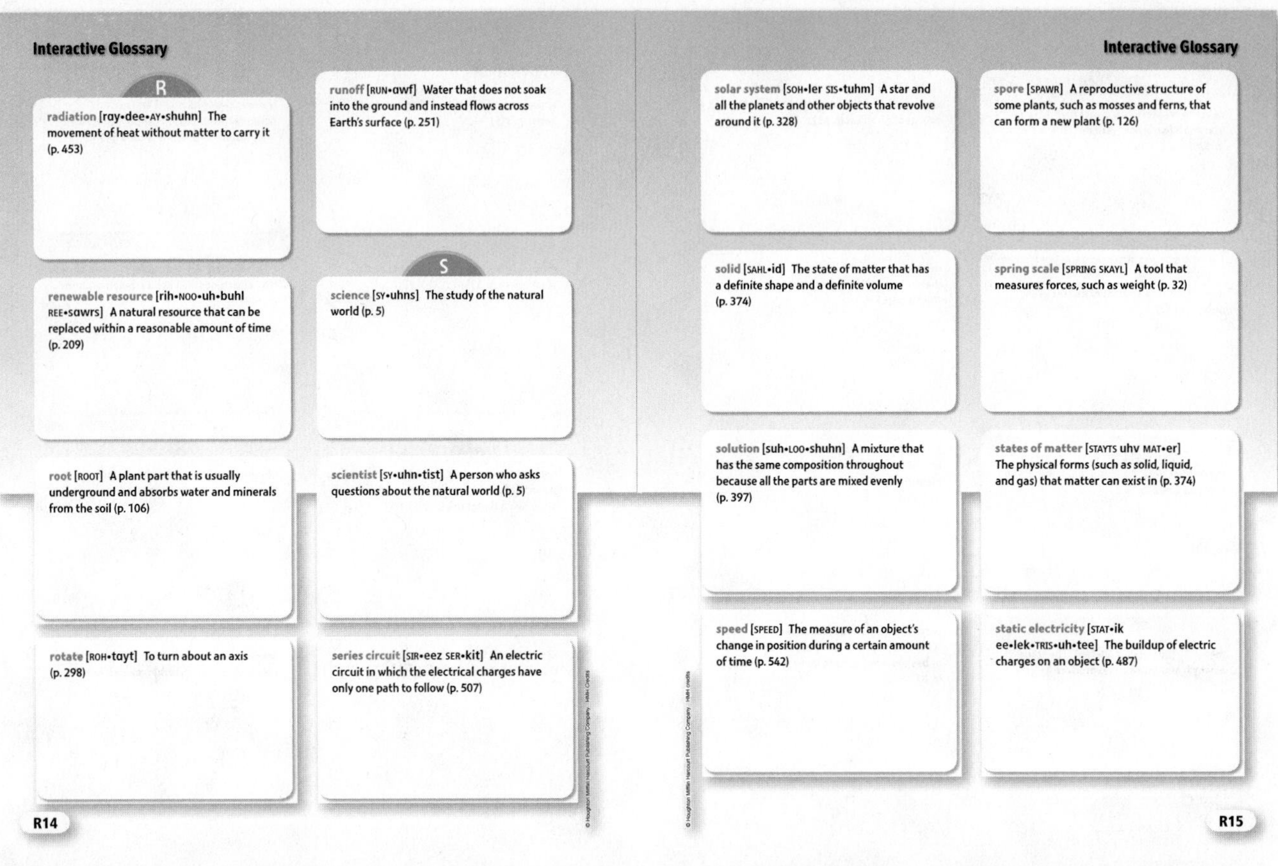

Interactive Glossary

R

radiation [ray•dee•AY•shuhn] The movement of heat without matter to carry it (p. 453)

renewable resource [rih•NOO•uh•buhl REE•sawrs] A natural resource that can be replaced within a reasonable amount of time (p. 209)

root [ROOT] A plant part that is usually underground and absorbs water and minerals from the soil (p. 106)

rotate [ROH•tayt] To turn about an axis (p. 298)

runoff [RUN•awf] Water that does not soak into the ground and instead flows across Earth's surface (p. 251)

S

science [SY•uhns] The study of the natural world (p. 5)

scientist [SY•uhn•tist] A person who asks questions about the natural world (p. 5)

series circuit [SIR•eez SER•kit] An electric circuit in which the electrical charges have only one path to follow (p. 507)

R14

Interactive Glossary

solar system [SOH•ler SIS•tuhm] A star and all the planets and other objects that revolve around it (p. 328)

solid [SAHL•id] The state of matter that has a definite shape and a definite volume (p. 374)

solution [suh•LOO•shuhn] A mixture that has the same composition throughout because all the parts are mixed evenly (p. 397)

speed [SPEED] The measure of an object's change in position during a certain amount of time (p. 542)

spore [SPAWR] A reproductive structure of some plants, such as mosses and ferns, that can form a new plant (p. 126)

spring scale [SPRING SKAYL] A tool that measures forces, such as weight (p. 32)

states of matter [STAYTS uhv MAT•er] The physical forms (such as solid, liquid, and gas) that matter can exist in (p. 374)

static electricity [STAT•ik ee•lek•TRIS•uh•tee] The buildup of electric charges on an object (p. 487)

R15

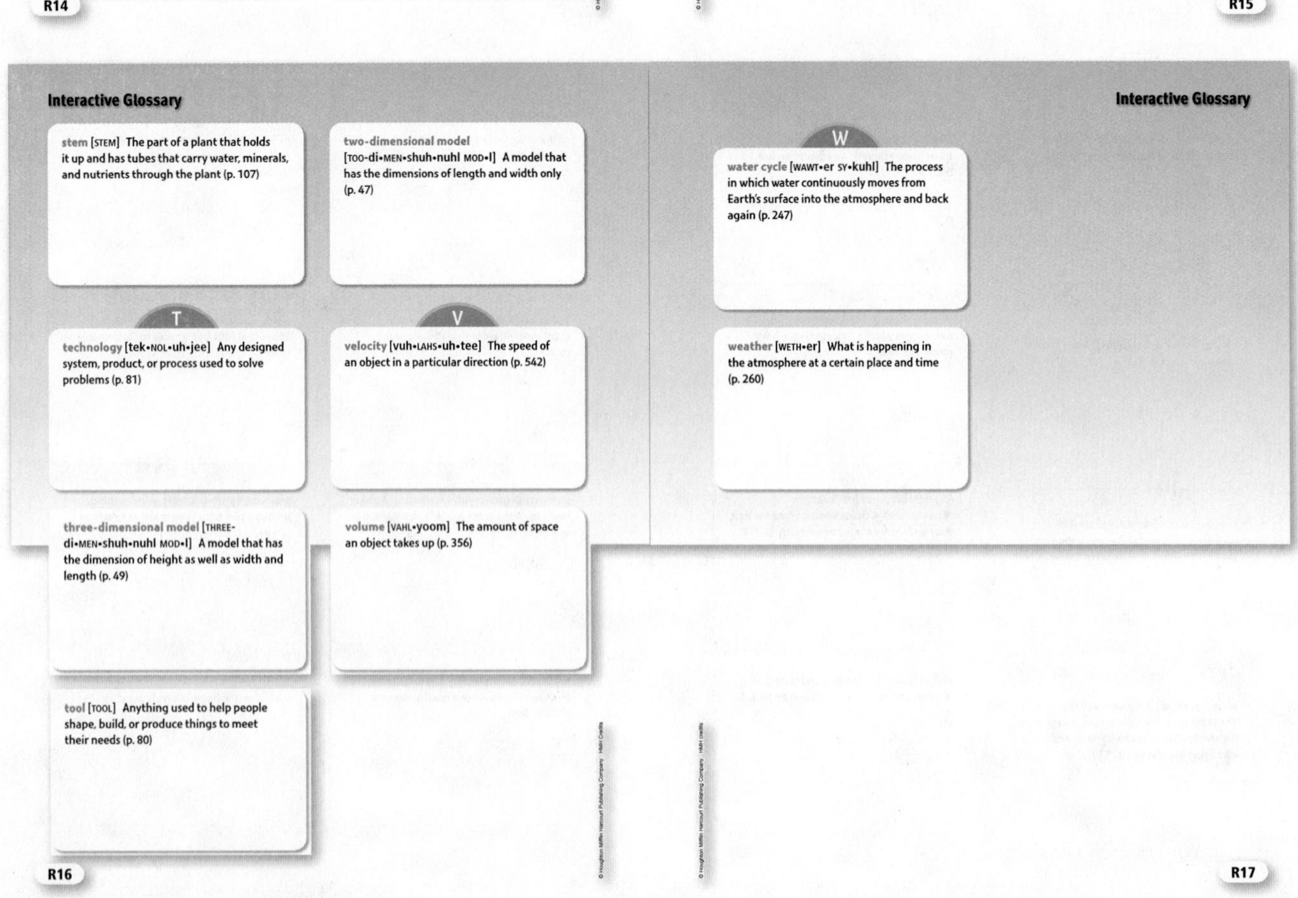

Interactive Glossary

stem [STEM] The part of a plant that holds it up and has tubes that carry water, minerals, and nutrients through the plant (p. 107)

T

technology [tek•NOL•uh•jee] Any designed system, product, or process used to solve problems (p. 81)

three-dimensional model [THREE-di•MEN•shuh•nuhl MOD•l] A model that has the dimension of height as well as width and length (p. 49)

tool [TOOL] Anything used to help people shape, build, or produce things to meet their needs (p. 80)

two-dimensional model [TOO-di•MEN•shuh•nuhl MOD•l] A model that has the dimensions of length and width only (p. 47)

V

velocity [vuh•LAHS•uh•tee] The speed of an object in a particular direction (p. 542)

volume [VAHL•yoom] The amount of space an object takes up (p. 356)

R16

Interactive Glossary

W

water cycle [WAWT•er SY•kuhl] The process in which water continuously moves from Earth's surface into the atmosphere and back again (p. 247)

weather [WETH•er] What is happening in the atmosphere at a certain place and time (p. 260)

R17

Index

Note: Page numbers in **boldface** indicate pages in the **Unit Teacher Editions.** PG pages refer to this *Planning Guide.* All other page numbers refer to pages in the *Student Edition,* which are reproduced in the Unit Teacher Editions.

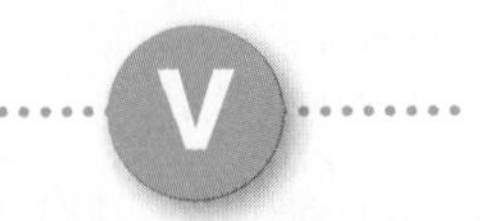

Y